BLUEPRINT FOR BUILDING COMMUNITY

LEADERSHIP INSIGHTS FOR GOOD GOVERNMENT

JOHN PERRY

Foreword by William F. Murphy

authorHOUSE®

AuthorHouse™
1663 Liberty Drive
Bloomington, IN 47403
www.authorhouse.com
Phone: 1-800-839-8640

First published by AuthorHouse   4/9/2010

ISBN: 978-1-4520-0627-7 (e)
ISBN: 978-1-4520-0625-3 (sc)
ISBN: 978-1-4520-0626-0 (hc)

Library of Congress Control Number: 2010904231

Printed in the United States of America
Bloomington, Indiana

This book is printed on acid-free paper.

TABLE OF CONTENTS

ACKNOWLEDGMENTS

This book results from the inspiration provided by the thousands of folks who have touched me during my career in public service. They contributed in so many ways to this book. I thank all of them for giving me the opportunity and support

Thanks to my twin brother Jim for encouraging me to get started and his editorial comments. Jim's colleague at Indiana University and retired city manger Orville Powell provided both encouragement and insight into the publishing process. My son Adam hosted me on St. Kitts for four months so that I had the solitude and time to devote to writing the manuscript. He was a steadying influence. My other son Jason provided extraordinary technical support.

I am grateful for the help from Woodridge staff, especially Leslie Davies, Peggy Halik, Katy Rush, and Melissa Bohse, who found documents that I needed for my research. Thanks also go to Greg Bielawski, John Joyce, and Phil Modaff for reading and commenting on the manuscript.

Mayor Bill Murphy has been a key contributor and steadying influence on my professional career, and a friend who would always listen. I am very proud that he authored the foreword.

My wife Pam supported my efforts to write this book. More importantly, she supported my work each day over the past four decades. She helped refine each chapter as it was lived.

FOREWORD

by William F. Murphy

Those who aspire to careers in public service, current managers, and elected officials, including mayors can benefit from the lessons of good governance shared by John Perry in the book "Blueprint for Building Community."

As the mayor of Woodridge, Illinois, for 30 years, John Perry stands out among the many outstanding managers and administrators I have worked with throughout the region, state and county. John Perry's credibility is a result of his academic background as a graduate of the University of Chicago and the Maxwell School of Syracuse University, coupled with his 37 years of service as an administrator in Park Forest, Illinois, and Woodridge, Illinois.

As a result of John Perry's leadership and management style during his service in Park Forest, the community was recognized as an All-America city, residential development, and economic development flourished and diversity was championed. During his tenure of 20 years in Woodridge, the property tax was reduced each and every year, and Woodridge was named as one of the "100 best small places to live" by Money magazine and "the world's greatest community-midwest" by the world's greatest tv show.

John Perry's management credibility and respect in the profession is also evidenced by his service as President of the Illinois City/county Management Association, as a founding member of the Illinois Public Employer Labor Relations Association, and as a founder and chairperson of the Intergovernmental Risk Management Association. At the time of his retirement, John Perry was selected by the Illinois City/county Management Association to receive the prestigious Robert B. Morris life time achievement award to recognize his outstanding contributions to the profession over the course of his career.

In the book "Blueprint for Building Community" you will learn leadership insights for good governance, strategies to build community and bedrock values and personal qualities that an aspiring manager, current manager, or elected official needs to build a community. The book is principle and lesson oriented with keys to forming an effective management team, ways to collaborate, and strategies for building communities and successful strategies in working with the community, elected officials, mayors, and staff.

In the book "Blueprint for Building Communities," John Perry has shared his perspective on what he did as a public administrator that contributed to his success and the success of the communities in which he served. The book is an outstanding opportunity for current administrators, aspiring professionals, elected officials and mayors to learn and revisit skills, strategies and leadership initiatives to do what is best for communities.

For me it also was a reaffirmation how fortunate Woodridge was to have John Perry as our leader and how fortunate I was to have him as a partner in good governance.

William F. Murphy, Mayor, Village of Woodridge

PREFACE

In each person's lifetime, there are experiences and feelings that you look back upon with wonder and amazement. We have all heard stories about "out of body" experiences. Those who have these transformative experiences are permanently refocused on life. I recently retired as village administrator of Woodridge Illinois. I now look back and sense the transformation that I experienced. I have been blessed to have had the opportunity to be a city manager. To my good fortune, I worked in communities that I could help and in the process they helped fulfill me. I have been changed by my experiences—all for the better. I have learned through the process and want to share the focus, and principles, that have become clearer through the prism of a career.

The pace of the last forty years has been hectic. A manager is advised to set aside time to reflect and absorb events that bombard him. Even if that advice were followed, there is even greater difficulty in also allocating meaningful time to recording and cataloging the events that shape one's life and documenting the conclusions and guidance that one gains from the experience. As the old adage goes "better late than never."

This book is my attempt to finally take the time to assess what has shaped my career, my development, and its impact on the communities which I have served. So, the first reason for writing this book is for me. I want to reflect on my work in a structured way. I have many thoughts, experiences and stories to share. I want to share my perspective on what I did---and why it has so influenced my life. I hope in doing so that I will improve my own grasp about the business of city management, and offer some insight for those who follow in my footsteps.

I also write this book as a tribute to the many people who have worked with me to build communities over the past four decades. Their vision, dedication, and sacrifice are inspirations to all professionals. Lastly, I hope to convey some of that inspiration, passion and excitement to all those who consider public service.

At the beginning of this book, I admit the difficulty I encounter in translating my experience. I begin with a reluctance to share my experience. First, I am not accustomed to the task of writing about what I do, or have done. In the course of my career, I didn't have time to devote significant time to recording what I had performed. Often what I did included many complex elements with many timelines before the results came together in an integrated way. The results may not also be fully discernible for months, years, or decades. Writing about these events and experiences are more the work of an historian than a village administrator.

Second, the purpose for which I served in Village government and for which I devoted my career was never about my work or experience. Public service is not a first person experience. My work and experience was about the work of many, the work of building community. My focus was about how the many and varied teams that make up the community work together. My efforts were always connected to the work of others. Being required to record these experiences and events in the first person is contrary to how I have viewed my role in the larger world since my youth.

So I humbly embark on the task of trying to analyze and convey the experiences of the past forty years. Henry Mintzberg in a 1975 Harvard Business Review article entitled *The Manager's Job: Folklore and Fact* argued that managers routinely are unable to articulate how the activities that they perform lead to the intended results. "What do managers do? Even managers themselves don't always know." Mintzberg strongly advocated the viewpoint that managers don't engage in a systematic program of planning, organizing, coordinating, and controlling. The "facts" he argued, based upon interviews and analysis of how managers spend time is not systematically related to these functions.

As I reflect on my own experiences, I am inclined to believe that managers do, or should, have a good sense of what they do and how these activities move their organizations and communities forward. Mintzberg's findings may be more related to asking the manager, who has been immersed in action, to precipitously "change gears" and reflect upon the work being done in a contemplative and analytical fashion. He may be capturing incomplete information because he's not making the assessment at the right time. I will try to share some principles that I learned in the course of my longer reflection and the feedback that I've gained over recent years. I hope that the readers will find these principles valuable.

FORMED BY MY HOMETOWN

City manager's experiences are molded by their environment. My reflections have caused me to relook at those formative years and how that experience molded me. I'm convinced that I came to the management profession partly because of my exposure while growing up with the city manager form of government in my hometown of Two Rivers, Wisconsin. I need to share some background on those early years because of the influence that they had on my choice of profession and what our profession must focus upon accomplishing.

I had uncles on both sides of the family that worked for the city, one as assessor and the other as recreation and parks director. They both spent their entire career working in municipal government. My parent's high school classmate, Hilary Rath, was the long time finance director for the city and eventually became city manager. I went to school with two of his sons with whom I participated on the track team. One of Hilary Rath's grandsons is now a city manager.

My primary recollections of city government were embedded in what I did from my first days venturing out of the neighborhood. I went to the supervised playground activities each summer to play baseball, checkers, caroms, tetherball, shuffleboard, and day camp at the state park. I went to the same park in the winter to participate at the supervised ice rink and warming shelter or the toboggan slide. On Thursday summer nights, my older sister took her twin brothers to the municipal band concert in central park. In the spring or fall, we might take archery lessons at the community house.

When I was ten, I had my appendix removed at the Two Rivers municipal hospital. We often accompanied my father when he visited family and friends at the nursing home and extended care facility. When my paternal grandfather and maternal grandmother died in 1956, we buried them in the "old" and "new" city cemeteries. When we went bowling, we often used the municipal lanes at the Community House. I learned basic mechanical drafting and wood-working at the municipal vocational school. My relatives used the same school to learn upholstery and leather tooling.

As a youngster, I didn't dwell on things like municipal water, municipal electricity, or municipal sewage treatment. Two Rivers city government had responsibility for all those functions too. As a formative teen, growing up under the JFK influence and interested in politics and government, I was surrounded during those early years by a shining example of how a comprehensive, efficient, low-key local government worked. You might say that I came to my profession through osmosis. I absorbed the impact of a community that had full service, real cradle-to-grave service.

During those formative years, my life was touched at every turn by the community that existed around me. I was impressed by what my hometown had accomplished as a community. The city manager sustained these facilities and programs that supported the community. I loved the community that first nurtured me.

PATHWAY TO A NEW COMMUNITY

My road out of Two Rivers took me to Chicago and the University located there that bears its name. I had little notion of the storied tradition of the University or its standing amongst the very best educational institutions in the world until I arrived for the on-campus orientation in September 1966. After two years exploring the "common core" of courses in philosophy, humanities, and western civilization, I chose the public affairs degree program, precursor for what is now the Harris School of Public Policy. I encountered many situations on-campus and in the city that shaped my outlook in terms of how government should support people. As a summer employee for the University, I participated in some of the early efforts to introduce citizen participation into neighborhood improvement programs.

After graduating in 1970, I performed my active service for the National Guard, got married, and headed off to the Maxwell School at Syracuse University to obtain my masters in public administration (MPA). I knew that an advanced degree was valuable to open doors, but I was eager to complete my education and begin my adult life, whatever that meant. I didn't have a grand plan. The masters program was an intense year. About half way through the program, I began to think about a JOB. I concluded based upon simple observation and the notion that higher level government was far removed from the people that I would be lost and unsatisfied in larger governments. I would explore the opportunities for local government and try to become a city manager.

By great luck, and the grace of God, I landed a job as assistant to the village manager in Park Forest, Illinois. I will begin my story about a career in city management with my arrival in Park Forest. It is a city that I served for 17 years eventually as city manager. I had the good fortune of serving only one other city, Woodridge Illinois. One of my peers in Park Forest called that village "god's town" and Woodridge was identified as the "world's greatest." I won't disagree with either designation. It was my good fortune to serve each of them. My good fortune may not be the norm, but luck plays a bigger part in our careers and subsequent "success" or "failure" than we might like to admit.

ORGANIZATION OF BOOK

This book is an analysis and synthesis of my personal experience. That personal experience is not a one-night affair. It is a journey that unfolded over four decades. I didn't always have guideposts. I think that I now know how Columbus felt on his first trip to the "New World." The only difference is that I've sighted land at the end of my journey—and I'm not disappointed by what I've found. Because of that long journey, however, I must map out information about the land--the communities which I'm exploring. On hindsight, I will offer analysis and insight that I did not necessarily see clearly the first time through. I would likewise encourage you not to see the communities through "2010 eyes" but to put yourself in the time and place described. This disclaimer might also help put the organization of my book in perspective.

This book is presented in ten chapters—too many for a person who emphasized brevity his whole career. Chapter One is a summary of philosophy and will outline the broad principles, themes, and strategies that I learned and practiced during my career. It will be a broad overview of the leadership principles needed to build communities. Chapter Two is that map of the journey or territory that I explored during my career. It contains background and history of the two communities in which I served and worked. These two communities, together with my hometown play a significant role in my conclusions for managing a community. I had a mentor who taught me lessons described in this chapter which I carried through the rest of my career. This chapter will identify some of the factors in my professional development and transformation of my perspective of the role of a city manager.

Chapter Three covers some of the bedrock values and personal qualities that a manager, or aspiring manager, needs to bring to his community. I might ascribe the values as those essential for public service. Additional personality traits are also described. These traits are highly desirable for a manager, but may be an element of the style of the individual and less universally applicable.

Chapter Four through Nine begin an elaboration of the skills, processes, strategy, and tactics which the manager must assemble to fulfill his role. Chapter Four concentrates upon the development of the partnership with the mayor and the molding of the team of elected officials. The manager must serve the elected officials as their primary resource. Providing sound, effective policy advice to the elected officials is a perquisite for the board to connect to the citizens. The unified leadership team will permit the manager to play a critical role to begin linking all the key players in the community.

Chapter Five is devoted to the elements of engaging the touchstone of community—citizens and stakeholders. The engagement elements of strategic management—community needs survey, town meeting, and neighborhood dialogues—will be explored. These engagement processes provide a structured basis for community building and involving employees in the engagement culture. Connections to the broader group of stakeholders, including business and governmental partners, cap the discussion of engagement in this chapter.

Chapter Six will expand on the strategies and processes that the manager should employ to accomplish the mission. The manager must find a way to achieve results for the community. I will describe the dynamic strategic management process in Woodridge that seeks to keep all the stakeholders focused on that mission. Results from the success of the strategic management process in Woodridge will be highlighted.

Chapter Seven examines the relationship of personal accountability that promotes leadership by each of the participants toward the mission of the community. Alignment of personal accountability with organization resources is the focus of real life stories that show how to translate this sense of responsibility to a "positive self-fulfilling prophecy." The key maxim to make sure that pathways to success are cleared and how "troublemakers" are isolated is also covered.

Chapter Eight consists of principles and attitudes that should drive the communications activities of the city organization and how to find connections to the community. The tools and media for communication will change, but the importance of knowing your audience, and how your message touches them is paramount.

Chapter Nine will be directed to my greatest passion--the building of the "team." I will explore the many components of assembling and developing the management team in this chapter. The objectives suggested in Chapter Nine are closely tied to building the larger village team envisioned in Chapter Four.

Chapter Ten is my opportunity to recap the lessons learned and the principles established. I will take the liberty of noting some of the personal experiences that gave me particular satisfaction. This closing chapter will also be my window to looking at the concerns and hopes for the future.

CHAPTER 1

FULFILLING DREAMS

The Last Lecture a video and book about Dr. Randy Pausch, a computer science professor, who died at 47 of pancreatic cancer, captured our hearts and spirits two years ago. The book had special meaning for me. I lost my sister to pancreatic cancer at 47. *The Last Lecture* is a story about fulfilling dreams and passing along some lessons for life. This book may never have the impact of Randy Pausch, but it is about fulfilling dreams, a tribute to those who shared them along the way, and some lessons for life.

"Life is a paradox." "Fact is stranger than fiction." "Never say never." All these catch phrases are a clear indication of the ironies of life. We just celebrated the 200th birthday of Abraham Lincoln; our most respected and admired President. Mr. Lincoln might find irony in being from Illinois, the state which competes for topping the list for all the values contrary to the Lincoln tradition. Lincoln brought honor to Illinoisans through his service and sacrifice. He stood for integrity, accountability, and commitment to country. Residents of Illinois would prefer to hold onto this ideal of leadership rather than what we have been dealt in state leaders in recent decades.

Adding to the irony, we have inaugurated a new President from Illinois. He is also our first African American President. Barack Obama has called for a commitment to a new generation of public service. He has asked for "our service and our active citizenship." The energizing of the younger generation has been quite impressive, and, hopefully, a harbinger of things to come. For some of us from the "older" generation, we welcome this renewal. For those of us who have committed our lives to public service since the 1960s, however, we see an irony in that we have continued to carry the "torch" and never have lost the fire of commitment to community.

While the national stage may see an ebb and flow to the value of public service, there is one arena in which that commitment to public service glows brightly. This arena is the community in which each of us calls home. While all politics is local, the governance and management of our communities are marked by a steadiness of purpose and service that sets them apart.

The philosophical swings of national politics have taken on cataclysmic proportions almost daily. Services at the community level continue unabated. A resident is burglarized, calls the police department, and an officer responds. A fire alarm triggers the engines to roll. Public Works sends the salt and plow trucks to clear the newly fallen 4" snow fall. You step into the shower in the morning and turn the faucet, the running water helps start your day. No, the shifts of national politics don't dramatically change what residents in our communities see happening each day and the continuing need to deliver these services.

Local government, the "lost" level of government in the federal system, still quietly goes about its business. Oftentimes, communities progress in spite of Washington policies. The steadiness and quality of our communities is a tribute to the contributions that elected officials, citizens, and professional staff make to building and maintaining our communities.

DeTocqueville, in his nineteenth century assessment of American life, considered local governments as the training ground for our democracy. The leadership challenge for communities, however, grows as resources diminish and the political polarization at higher levels of government does nothing to address local needs. We need to better understand why and how we come together at the community level to best serve our residents.

For thirty seven years I have been immersed in the dynamic profession of city management. As I reflect on my career and the outstanding people and opportunities that have been part of that experience, I hope to share the insights that may guide communities—their elected officials, residents, and professional managers—through the difficult challenges ahead. I will briefly describe in this book the why, who, and what associated with the best practices that I observed during my thirty seven year career.

What is the purpose of our work in local government? Work in local government is distinctive from work at the state and federal levels. There is an intimacy and closeness at the community level that is different from the connection at any other level of government. President Obama wants to renew the citizen connection—but must rely upon media that are more distant, less interactive, and unable to simultaneously convey the mutuality of emotions present. Whether the city manager encounters residents at a public hearing, the local grocery store, or down the street from his home, the city manager is there in person. The city manager is connected in time and space to the citizen. The city manager is always "available" and at hand.

The setting and environment of the work for the city manager is different from state and federal government work. You are directly accountable, personally present, each and every day. The local government manager is working in the environment originally conceived for bringing people together in community. Early Greek models for democracy were built on a small scale around the notion that all citizens were actively involved in the affairs of the city. This opportunity to build a community that fulfills the early ideals of community, providing for the basic well-being of the citizens and the environment where they could develop their full potential as people uniquely belongs to those who work in local government.

Broadly, three elements shape the success of the city manager in building community. First, the manager needs to grasp the aspirations of the community served. Second, the manager needs to demonstrate the values that build confidence in the role that he fulfills in the community. Third, he must find ways to link and connect all the community stakeholders and support their aspirations. The remainder of this chapter will expand on these three elements and close with one real-life example of how these elements played out in Woodridge.

City Management—The Sacred Responsibility

This responsibility for building community is a uniquely local business and its chief professional is the city manager. The Oath of the Athenian City

State echoes the call that we must still heed: "We will fight for the ideals and Sacred Things of the City both alone and with many." The obligation that we carry is to "fight" for the "ideals and sacred things of the city." We must work to build communities that fulfill this charge. City managers sometimes get lost in the question of efficiency. Efficiency may be on the manager's list, but that is not where our work starts. Why we do the work of a city manager is to add purpose and meaning to the lives of people who come together in a community. Our purpose is the purpose of the people in our city.

If we believe in this purpose for our work, we must subscribe to a set of values that honors the tradition of building community. I put three values in the foundation for building the community—trust and faith, integrity, and respect. The twin values of trust and faith are at the very heart of our work. We must have trust and faith in the "wisdom of the masses." We come together in community because we are trying to become a cohesive unit to support the members of the group. The city manager must nurture the work of the many to provide opportunities for each member of the community. For it is in connecting to others that we all become better.

The city manager first needs to show trust and faith in himself—and view all those around him with the same regard. Without trust and faith in elected officials, citizens, and employees, the city manager can not make all the connections required to build an outstanding community. He can not call for the help that is needed to build the dreams of the citizens and the community collectively without trust and faith. The essence of building community is establishing mutual trust with all the stakeholders and nurturing that faith and trust on a daily basis.

The second foundation value is integrity. If we want to pursue the sacred things of the city, then we must not do anything that will "dishonor" that pledge. We all understand the complexities of communicating to the many stakeholder groups. We must make efforts to not only tell the truth, but make sure that we educate all these stakeholder groups in a manner that will help them fulfill their roles. City managers agree that our most important professional distinction is the Code of Ethics to which we commit. Our successful application of this Code goes far beyond "telling the truth." We have to communicate to our boards and citizens so that our individual role and our collective effort to build community have credibility.

Respect is the third value in our foundation for community building. We must increase the "reverence and respect" for those with whom we work to build community. If you have trust and faith in others, you best demonstrate those twin values by including a role for all who participate in building community. To do otherwise, defeats the very purpose of community building and why our profession exists.

These three foundation values are part of your basic mores for you to carry out your tasks as city manager. You will also require many personal skills to navigate during your community building journey. Value-based leadership in your community that fits with, and supports your style, will make a tremendous difference in the outcome. Values must be supported by actions that live those values. What better place to live those actions than in our communities.

Cherish the Uniqueness of Your Community

You show the value of the "ideals and sacred things" of the city by learning about your community and respecting its unique character and history. The citizens who come together in community first want to see your commitment to what they have built. It is in the understanding of the community foundation and the hopes for its future development that you begin your service as manager. From this understanding, you will need to work to establish the mission that will become the "self-fulfilling prophecy." The manager needs to figure out the dreams of the community and help move the community in the direction of making them come true. These are the "ideals and sacred things" that gives the manager a purposeful role. He needs to find a way for the other stakeholders to become involved in building the community of the future on the foundation of the present. The city manager nurtures that keystone of trust and faith through the absolute commitment to the community.

Everyone Needs to Help Build Community

Citizens are the ultimate touchstone for all that we do. We need to enlist them in helping to build the community. Community building is everyone's job. The first step is to confirm that there is an understanding of the mission—the "self-fulfilling prophecy" that brings folks together. We then need to insure that all are committed to that mission. We need to find ways to communicate with them and ask them how we can move toward our mission—and how each of us will contribute.

The city manager is the link between governing board and employees. The mayor, board, and manager is the core management team that must work together to coalesce the efforts of the community. At the core of this top management team is the mayor/manager partnership. This partnership is the leader team that sets the bar for the city organization and rallies the community to work together. These two leaders working in partnership want to bring all into the endeavor of building community.

The city manager is the primary resource for the mayor and the elected officials. He needs to "make them look good," not in a superficial way, but as the group responsible for governing the community. The elected officials must project leadership for the mission and goals of the community and as symbol for the "ideals and sacred things" that brings the community together. The city manager will work to point all toward the mission that the community has set and how progress can be made toward that vision. Building community is about building capacity amongst this core management team—the board as the governing body and the staff as generators of options to "make things happen" as well as the implementers of the designated action steps. The city manager must work to connect the management team to the board and to the residents and other stakeholders. We are better as a community by connecting to each other.

Teamwork for the Super Bowl

What needs to be done to make sure that community building becomes everyone's job? You will need to grow the team, one player at a time. Community building is incremental. It is constant. It does not end. We built a process in Woodridge that we called strategic management. This process which evolved over time melded together the components that were necessary to bring together all the stakeholders in the community.

Citizen Engagement

The elected officials provide leadership that steadfastly focuses on the village mission. In their wisdom, the Woodridge mayor and trustees recognized that citizen engagement, a real voice and real role for stakeholders, had to be part of building community.

Citizen engagement does not happen by accident. A community must design processes and structures to make effective connections to stakeholders. This helps send the message that input is valued. Woodridge has a long tradition of surveying residents to evaluate the community and its services. We added to that tradition neighborhood dialogues, town meeting, and other special task forces to focus upon the mission and how citizens could work with us for its achievement. We were successful because citizen input had a visible impact upon our activities, projects, and mission.

Citizen engagement is not just practiced by the governing body. Employees have a major role. They have more contact with residents each day than any board member has in a year. All those employee service contacts give us the opportunity to build a citizen engagement culture from the "outside in." Employees must be empowered to geometrically add to the connections of residents to the community.

Citizen engagement is the basis for defining the village mission, and the basis for insuring its pursuit. Each community has a set of "corporate" stakeholders as well. As the state with the most units of government, we in Illinois have a particular need to include other units of government, park district, school district, fire district, and library. The missions of each of these organizations must reinforce and support the community's mission.

Manager Must Help All Fulfill Dreams

The manager's job is to find a way for all those who become engaged in the community to fulfill the dreams that are defined for the community. He needs to translate the mission into a "positive self-fulfilling prophecy" for each participant. The manager must find a way to achieve results. I consider myself intelligent, but the manager's job is not to be smart. He needs to first and foremost help everyone else.

The manager must lead his professional team to develop strategies and options that will move the community toward its mission—and maintain the focus on the mission. City managers have been entrusted with carrying out the mission—the ideals and sacred things of the city. Managers who pass along that trust and faith to the department directors will be most successful. Managers must "radiate" leadership for community goals to those people that they make responsible for daily operations—the directors who instill and support employees in the citizen engagement culture. The city manager sets the bar to make the director group the operational leaders, bench markers, strategists, educators, communicators, and leaders for achievement of the goals and mission of the community.

This professional management team is the core group to link the goals, set by the community through its elected officials, to measurable results. All those involved in the community building process must have good data—data to assess progress, data to judge options, data to measure efficiency. Good data is essential to making good decisions. Good data helps educate everyone involved in the strategic management process and stay grounded in reality, not fantasy. Good data is critical to establishing and maintaining credibility that supports the foundation for trust and faith.

Community Self-Evaluation

Elected officials, citizens, and employees work together to achieve the mission—build the community. These participants must routinely monitor their progress, collectively and as sub-groups. Woodridge evaluates the city manager, the city manager evaluates the department manager, and department managers evaluate their employees, and so on. The assessment does not stop with these paid employees. The citizens evaluate the community and service performance, elected officials and staff evaluate the strategic management process annually, and town meeting brings together 200 friends and neighbors to assess community progress. The effective community, a successful community regularly focuses upon progress toward its mission—and realistically evaluates its status and condition.

Michael Briand in a 1998 article in the National Civic Review entitled *Five Principles for a Community That Works* summarizes why some communities work:

"...Communities that work are ones in which there's a well established practice of participation and cooperation. People are able to talk, think, and act together. This pragmatic readiness of people to work together enables such communities to meet their fundamental responsibility of responding effectively to needs, problems, and opportunities over time. In short, communities that work are good at making sound decisions that lead to effective action."

Briand identifies five principles that the Heartland Center for Leadership Development distilled from successful communities—inclusion, comprehension, deliberation, cooperation, and realism. My own experience confirms the importance of these leadership and citizen engagement factors. Effective, committed professionals will support the link between elected leadership and citizens, because therein lies the opportunity for the professional to achieve mastery in serving the community.

Town Center Plan Proves Community Building Philosophy

What are the results when you identify community aspirations pursue them with valued leadership, and support these aspirations with the resources and teamwork of the community? Starting in 2004, Woodridge became involved in a major public policy dispute with the local high school district (District 99). The history of that dispute provides several mileposts for the road to effective community building. Let me use that story to briefly highlight elements that contribute to community building that will be highlighted in the chapters ahead.

In the 1970s, Woodridge established a plan to make its geographic center a Town Centre, which included a variety of public and institutional uses. In 1978, District 99 annexed a key parcel in the heart of the Town Centre to the fledgling village and envisioned its use as a third high school site. The Village agreed to the annexation and prospective use subject to a letter of commitment from the district that the Village would have the opportunity to purchase the property ("right of first refusal") if it were not used as a high school. Beginning in 1971, the Woodridge park district leased the property for community recreation and open space use. Prior to 2004, voters in the high school district three times rejected funding for a third high school.

Concurrent with the district's "high school planning" process, the residents of Woodridge gathered in annual town meetings to evaluate the Woodridge mission and our progress in achieving the mission. Over a five year period starting in 1999, the feedback from residents voiced increased interest for the village to consider the impacts of development and saving more open space, a dwindling community resource. In 2002, given continuing feedback from residents at the town meeting, village officials began exploring acquisition of the district site with school district officials. The school board president and superintendent assured village officials that the district was ready to honor the commitment made when the site was annexed and they would respond to the village's interest after further planning review, particularly athletic field needs.

The interest in open space became a priority issue for evaluation in 2003 through the strategic management process. Village staff evaluated parcels in Woodridge to assess the quality and cost for sites as open space. The mayor and the board used the options provided by the staff to set priorities for future preservation and acquisition. Staff eventually translated the Board priorities into a financial plan for acquiring the properties. The park district which had used this site for several decades, and participated in planning for its future, actively partnered with the village. These village efforts to respond to the town meeting feedback were shared with residents at each opportunity for citizen engagement and communication. The community was engaged in actions to successfully fulfill its mission.

District 99 conducted more studies on the site, but did not respond to the village about the terms for acquisition. Hoping to avoid addressing the issue, the district chose to ask tax payers for an increase in taxes. District taxpayers soundly rejected the request. After the failed election, the superintendent promised the village administrator that the district would sit down with the village to discuss valuation of the property following some more homework. The administrator provided the district with historical information about the property, its zoning, and appraisals that had been previously commissioned.

When the deadline for meeting by the superintendent passed, and passed again, without a plausible explanation, the administrator asked the village attorney to review the village's authority to condemn the property. Both the administrator and attorney knew that the law generally did not permit such condemnations of one taxing body's property by another without express statutory authority.

This was an important community issue, however, and all options had to be determined. Somewhat surprisingly, the attorney found that statutory authority. The administrator briefed the mayor and the board that an option did exist for the village and park district to protect the village's plan for a town centre devoted to open space and public uses. No Illinois municipal government had ever exercised that statutory authority.

The village learned just three weeks later after late night closed door action by the district and a large real estate ad in the *Wall Street Journal* that the district wanted to sell the parcel for multi-family housing. The district chose not to cooperate with the village, nor live by the good faith commitment to sell the property if it were not used as a third high school. The village convened more than two hundred residents to discuss how the district's decision impacted the village and the long term vision for a town centre anchored by public uses and open space. Residents were angered by the district's lack of truthfulness and good faith. The community was firmly behind its long time plan. The Village had to condemn the parcel.

The village did condemn the property in May 2005. In 2007, a judge ruled that the village had the authority to condemn the property. A year later, a jury set the price at $14 million. The village paid for the property and now shares control of the parcel with the park district. The district has appealed the court's decision.

How does this experience reflect the principles of building community that this book will address in greater detail? The community had a long term plan. It was confirmed formally by the elected officials in 1970, 1971, 1978, 1985, 1993, 1995....many more times than I care to recap. Key stakeholders were engaged as well. The park district cooperated with the village for decades; when the issue reached critical stage, the park district was a partner—co-leader. This issue coalesced as a result of citizen engagement through the town meeting. Those community conversations produced a comprehension by all participants that (1) open space was important; (2) balanced growth of the economic base also required preservation of some open space; and (3) the community had prudently managed its finances, reserving money for open space acquisition. All participants--elected officials, citizens, and employees--could "pat themselves on the back" for having the capacity to act on their dreams in building community.

The commitment to town centre was established through steadfast elected leadership and citizen engagement. That commitment was supported through unprecedented work by staff in providing options to the community planning process. These options were routinely part of the planning process that spanned 1970-2005. As the time for action neared, the staff generated options to purchase specific properties. The board through the citizen engagement process set priorities.

The staff worked on financial plans to carry out these options. The staff, including outstanding participation by the village attorney, had options available to the board provided the district chose not to cooperate with the village plans. When the district chose to impair the village plan, the Woodridge community followed through on its plans for building the community as envisioned. The community team was ready for each opportunity and had a contingency plan for each option.

The village actions were public at each step of the way, girded by significant public participation. The village pursued its mission and the "self-fulfilling prophecy." The village actions supported building community and were underpinned by basic values of trust and faith, respect, and integrity. The stature of the community, its elected officials, citizens, and employees were enhanced by how this matter was addressed. What perhaps is most impressive is the longevity of the village plan and the sustained commitment and perseverance in pursuing it. Unfortunately, Woodridge was not able to engage the district to pursue a mutually effective solution without litigation.

In the chapters ahead, I will provide more specifics about how we gained this successful result and many more. I will also share more about the journey that helped me understand the principles for success.

CHAPTER 2

A PLACE TO CALL HOME

It is all about community. I do not need a long script to tell this story. Community is something that you do. "Just do it!" is the best way to learn about building community. I so enjoyed being involved in the community building work that I would encourage you to try it! In the interest of whetting your appetite for the challenge, I will provide you the long version of my "script" detailing what you might find if you take this journey.

This chapter is intended to be the backgrounder for two things. First, I want us to have a common set of facts about the communities in which I worked—Park Forest and Woodridge. Second, my early experiences taught me some lessons, and generated some biases, that are tied to the principles that will be discussed later in this book. I would like you to be able to follow the facts that are behind my conclusions.

The principles that are discussed later in this book are most often placed in the context of Woodridge experiences. However, you need to see how my earlier experiences in Park Forest shape my personal development. Any successes that I enjoyed in Woodridge came from my education in Park Forest. This community background may in some way also be helpful in delineating how I learned and built upon my management experiences to become a better professional.

Make Sure That Professional Commitment Profits the Community

You may be reading this book to learn the "general" principles to be a "good" manager. I hope to convey some of those general guides for how our profession can be more successful. The first point is that it is not about the "general" principles. It is about community—the distinctiveness of each one—their unique character. The story of the two communities in which I served helps to make the point that understanding and appreciating the character of each community is an essential prerequisite for managing successfully within the community.

Each community is distinctive. We are in the business of public service. Our business needs to turn a "profit." I am being somewhat facetious in using the word "profit." I am not at all talking net cash flow. We need to focus upon investing in our business to enhance its long term value. Our "Boards of Directors" need to have the same focus. The manager who focuses upon community building and its "profit" will enjoy his circumstances and be less concerned about advancement and career progression. We need those who observe our work as seeing our profession as profiting from how we build the business of community.

I hope that the background and story of my two communities will highlight their special and unique character and the importance of managing with this principle as the top priority. In the remainder of this chapter, I will provide background first on Park Forest. I will conclude that background with the guidelines and lessons earned from that experience. Next I will turn to Woodridge's early history and the foundations that were set by that community before I arrived in 1989.

Park Forest: A Post-War New Town

By great luck, and the grace of God, I started my career as assistant to the village manager in Park Forest, Illinois. My new boss was Bob Pierce, an Oklahoma educated MPA with twenty years experience, the last ten years in Park Forest. He was from the "old school," emphasizing the role of the manager, especially in the Illinois statutory form. Despite the authority of the manager's role, he realized that this is democratic government and emphasized its supremacy. Above all, he realized that the one element that distinguished the form, and the manager occupying the position, is an absolute commitment to personal integrity and the manager's support for honest and open governance of the community and all its stakeholders. Part of his "old school" philosophy was that he hired department managers and "let them do their job."

Although Bob Pierce was "old school," he had openness to innovation and cutting-edge community programs, like supporting racial integration, youth, and health services. These programs were not the mainstay of municipal activities anywhere in 1970.

My landing in Park Forest was another stroke of good fortune. I landed in my first community, but not an ordinary community. This community definitely had its own personality and character. A community, like each person, wants to be recognized for its individuality, what it stands for, and what it wants to ideally become. The history of Park Forest was a tribute to its uniqueness.

Park Forest—A Recipe from Scratch

Park Forest didn't exist in 1946. It is the prototypical post-World War II planned community. Development began in 1947, led by former Federal Housing Authority Commissioner Philip Klutznik, Lewis Manilow, and Sam Beeber. The compact five square mile parcel of real estate that became Park Forest was on the outer edge of south suburbia. The Chicago Northwestern Railway, a primary artery to the University of Chicago and the Chicago Central Business District, runs along the western edge of the community. Few resources were available to build housing during World War II. However, the GI in the post-war economy was not only returning home and to "private life," but desperately in need of affordable housing as he began civilian life --and resuming family-life and raising children.

The developers laid out a plan for how the community would develop and began construction in 1947. The plan called for about 10,000 units of affordable housing. The initial 3,000 units of row houses configured around back porches on the parking court and the front facing significant expanses of green space. The remaining 7000 units were single-family residences on lots averaging 6000 square feet, mostly on slabs without basements due to the topography and soil hydrology. A "planned" community that sold itself as providing for the needs of returning vets needed more than homes to be attractive to the returning vets who wanted the best for their families.

The developer's plan called for school sites to serve each neighborhood and the many children who were to soon follow. Many of these school sites were combined with park land set aside for future recreational purposes. There was also a 90 acre central park, much of it undevelopable, which adjoined other central sites set aside for commercial and community facilities. Families needed to buy the necessities and commercial areas were provided for that. Families also attended church. Five sites were laid out for future churches. Although most of the early Park Forest population commuted to Chicago, the developer also provided an industrial park for future businesses.

High Growth Redefined

Thus, early Park Forest was planned to provide for all the necessities of post World War II family and community life. The developers found that their objectives were met with great excitement and prospective residents turned out in huge numbers. The community added residents at about 2500 per year for its first 12 years. Few communities in the Chicago area have enjoyed that pace of growth since. Park Forest had a population of over 30,000 by 1960, just twelve years after its incorporation.

Formative Expectations

The genesis for Park Forest, unique in the character of its initial development, had an even more profound impact on the expectations and collective will of the people which it attracted. The residents of this "new" community, who made the commitment to locate in the early days, also believed that there should be other changes in the expectations for how a community was run and how it served those same residents. First order of business was for the early residents to take over the operation of the community. Klutznik, in his early recollections of the town's formation, provided the following perspective,

> "We have realized two things from the start, one is that no matter how much planning goes into a project like this, it will only be judged by results. The other is that no matter

how much work and time we have spent, the people who live there can form the spirit and character we have sought for it. We all feel that unless the town-hall spirit in which Park Forest was created is captured and held by the people we will have failed. This is our gamble. We're betting on the people."

Klutznik, also the developer of Oak Brook Center, Old Orchard, and Water Tower Place, was a visionary of his time. He had amazing business acumen for building homes—and building community. Klutznik set the tone for his new residents and trusted that they had the interest and ability to run the village government. He took the risk of "walking the talk." In early 1949, only a year into Park Forest's development, the residents and developer collaborated to incorporate the community and turn its governance over to the residents.

People like Jack Meltzer, a pre-eminent urban planner and later Director of the University of Chicago's Center for Urban Studies for whom I worked as a student in 1968, were representative of the quality leadership that served on the village board during those early years. The community's early leadership abided by a simple philosophy--we are a new community, started in a new way, and we need to provide for a society that is not following in the footsteps of the past. In some ways, you might say that these early village pioneers wanted to establish a "whole, new world." Many of the early community initiatives reflected this notion.

Early Pioneers--Respect Through Living Together

Early government initiatives covered a broad spectrum of subjects. One of the areas that have been the focus of Park Forest government activity since the first days of the community has been an emphasis on human relations--how people <u>should</u> treat each other. A significant part of the early settlers in Park Forest were Jewish and Japanese Americans. The events and atrocities surrounding World War II were clear in their minds.

There was a collective desire on the part of the residents to actively combat human disrespect and encourage good relationships amongst all. In 1951, residents petitioned the board of trustees to establish an advisory commission on human relations. This group which was formalized three years later would play a significant role throughout the decade in discussing racial conflicts and exploring how housing accessibility could be improved for all races.

In the Chicago area formal and open tools to control and manipulate race and perpetuate segregation existed into the 1960s. The unwritten rules that promoted steering, block-busting, and panic-peddling were even more pernicious and longer lasting. In the mid-1950s the first black family trying to move to town encountered neighborhood resistance and aborted the effort. Through the efforts of a local church group and the commission on human relations the first African American family moved to the village in 1959 without incident.

Community leaders established the practice of meeting with neighbors of black families about integration. The process of communicating with residents about integration through the commission on human relations and local churches and synagogues made people more comfortable with integration. The village government, at the same time, made a strong effort to make minority families feel welcome and insured that all persons would receive equal protection and services.

Distinction through Caring and Citizen Action

A project that had special significance for the community in its early days was the construction of the Aqua Center. This 50,000 square foot complex, consisting of four pools, was a center piece of community life for the many youth and adults in the fledgling community. One of the unusual aspects of its development that still amazes me is that it was built privately by a group of residents that came together and financed the facility through $100 bonds sold to prospective members. Until 1974, the Aqua Center was run by a board of community volunteers.

Another unusual, although not unique, undertaking by the community shortly after incorporation involved establishing a health department. The health department provided many services, including providing school nursing services under contract to school district 163 (SD 163).

Volunteer Spirit Produces All-America City

As a new community with a rapidly increasing population, schools were an important matter for early attention. The developer had planned for grade schools which became school district 163. However, there was no high school to serve the residents. They set about to establish a new high school district and build a new facility near the center of the community. For their efforts in this project and other evidence of the "can do" spirit, the community was named an All-America City in 1954, a designation emblematic of volunteer participation in community life.

The character of the community, whether by necessity of the circumstances or by that unique American crucible process, came together early and distinguished itself for the values that were collectively represented by its residents. This spirit for which the community has become well-known has been its source of strength. This same independent spirit has been a challenge for the leadership over the last three decades to undertake change in the plan that was established years ago

Perils for an Aging Community

As the community has aged, what are the issues that present challenges for sustaining the ideals and character of the community into the future? Since the 1970s, Park Forest has experienced several impacts from changes in the mode of transportation.

Transportation modes change. Park Forest has encountered the threat of decreasing importance of rail transportation and the concomitant rise of the automobile. These shifts in transportation behaviors have been most significant for purposes of determining the primary grid that would carry people back and forth to jobs and shopping. The location advantage for the Park Forest of the 1950s--central city with fixed rail access--would diminish as time progressed. Location on a network of highways that served automobile traffic would become increasingly important. Traffic routes would first play a role in reducing the prominence of Park Forest Plaza. The Plaza became a significant regional shopping center because it got a head start in the 1950s and 60s on that genre of shopping facility. The Plaza, located on a minor arterial, and other specialty retailers, including auto dealers, would likewise be diminished by the inexorable movement toward retail power centers and the location of retailers along high traffic arterials and interstates.

Tax base not keeping pace. The original plan for Park Forest had limited space for non-residential development. As the community entered the 1980s, this lack of a diversified tax base to pay for the costs of government services, especially schools, became more evident. The community had responded to support for schools at five tax referendum which pushed the tax rate above $12 per hundred EAV.

During my time in Park Forest, I saw the steady progression of one of the most insidious property taxation and assessments systems in the country. In the early 1970s, Cook County received authority to classify property for the purpose of taxing at differential rates, i.e., single family, commercial, multi-family rental, etc. Higher tax rates for non-residential development have shifted a greater percentage of the tax burden to that type of development. Those non-residential developments, wherever possible, have fled Cook County. There are now more than a dozen classes of taxation. These classes have resulted from political solutions to tax equity issues and have driven considerable development from Cook County. For communities like Park Forest, which is a short distance from Indiana, this system has been especially adverse to business attraction. The remaining taxable development in Cook County, residential and non-residential alike ends up paying a higher tax rate and higher taxes due to the reduction in the size of the aggregate tax base.

A Bittersweet Start to My Manager Term

When I became acting village manager in late 1982, I was not coming into a situation with which I was unfamiliar, nor were the challenges facing the community unknown. There had been considerable conflict and tension in the months that preceded my ascending to the manager position, much of it revolving around my predecessor and mentor. As a result, there had been much energy expended without any results for moving the community forward. The mayor Ron Bean was a man of substantial talent. His election itself is evidence of the regard in which he was held by the community. He had been elected the prior year as the first African-American mayor--in a community with only 14 percent minority population.

Mayor Bean enjoyed modest support on the board of trustees. He had a vision for the community and Park Forest's role in the broader south suburban region. He was ready to act more aggressively and take on greater risks than the village had been willing to undertake during the prior decade. He saw the village as a major partner with the private sector in rejuvenating and financing the Plaza and other initiatives. Following the mid-1970s, Park Forest did not have a track record for consensus being a priority. If there was a consensus, it was that Park Forest placed a priority on each person's opinion and citizen participation oftentimes characterized by a long process of public input without conclusion. If results were achieved, that was a plus for the process, but a process of discussion was paramount.

Investment is Essential

By late 1982 the history of village political conflict in recent years had slowed positive results for the community. The mayor and a majority of the trustees saw that strengthening the economic base of the community was sorely needed. This was the mindset as I began development of my first budget and action plan. The city manager needs to help move the community forward whenever the opportunity arises. My opportunity was at hand and I wasn't in a position to go through an extended consensus building process.

I organized my action plan around the theme of investment in the community. There are many avenues for investment and the manager needs to find those that are acceptable politically and move the community forward. We will regularly return to this principle of the manager being a catalyst for producing results that invest in building community for the long term.

If a community is going to sustain itself, it must be able to attract sufficient investment to maintain the "infrastructure" that it has. I saw investment being required in four areas of community infrastructure--(1) housing; (2) citizen participation; (3) government services; (4) economic base. The specific types of investment needed to sustain a community will differ, depending upon the age and circumstances of a community. The manager's job is to help the community assess what resources are available and how those resources can be allocated to maximize the investment in community. The key nuance here may be obtaining agreement on what resources are "available" and everyone understanding the reality of what can be accomplished.

Budget Strategies 1983 Style

For each of the above areas of investment, I tried to focus on proposing budget strategies that would help build the community for the future. Since resources were particularly dear, I built incremental allocations for new investments around the Peter Drucker concept of "sloughing off" those activities that no longer generated benefits for the community. For housing infrastructure, Park Forest, with little room for expansion, needed to assure that its housing was well-maintained through investment by existing homeowners. The village placed a high priority on code enforcement as the "stick" that would further this investment.

While citizen participation was long a hallmark of village government, the Park Forest of the 1980s had come to rely upon standing committees who often had to "find something to do." There were many opportunities for investments in this infrastructure, particularly contributions from residents on an ad hoc basis that could be pursued to maintain the vibrancy of citizen participation.

The expenditures by village government need to emphasize the value that each service brings to the community's quality of life. Are there infrastructure investments that the community can make to spur non-residential development? These types of government services can assist the private sector with the need for investment in the economic base. Each community must also look to what investments that might be made to expand the tax base. The 1980s were a period in municipal government when the concept of public-private partnership took hold and grew exponentially.

Early Months at the Helm

My first months as manager were very exhilarating. The village board and staff were eager and poised to act. The mayor, one trustee and I ventured off to Winnipeg Canada the week before my youngest son was born. We were trying to learn from the lender what options existed for redeveloping the Park Forest Plaza which was in the midst of its second foreclosure in recent years. We were also rapidly closing in on finalizing a redevelopment for a neighborhood shopping center which would bring a Dominick's food store to town. The Park Forest Aqua Center, now operated by the YWCA, was set to shutter. The board encouraged staff to find a solution for making sure that this venerable community facility continued in operation.

On all investment fronts—housing, economic development, infrastructure, village programs supporting integration, and citizen participation— we made significant progress that first year. The staff had board and community support to take some actions that were long sought. The Park Forest Plaza came under new ownership and grants were obtained to assist refurbishing the facility. We came up with assistance and a financing plan for the Dominick's project. Special code enforcement efforts spurred progress at a major multi-family development.

Aqua Center Revived

Perhaps the most instructive project that first year was the successful acquisition of the Aqua Center. This project was my best opportunity to facilitate employee and citizen engagement. We negotiated a tentative agreement to acquire the facility from the YMCA. We confirmed the terms with the village board. Money was dear and we could not afford to use general sources of taxation. We bought the facility with no cash upfront and assumed the remaining bonded indebtedness from the original bondholders of about $35,000. A key component was enlisting the support of employees and community members to volunteer services to clean-up and refurbish the facility to get it open in a month. We shared our needs with employees first. They were excited to have the opportunity to help. We could "roll" the plan out to the residents who were also excited to be able to see the facility reopen. Citizens and employees contributed nearly 1000 hours of volunteer support to reopen this facility. We asked for help with a project that was important to the public. We got the help needed from key stakeholders to be successful.

Still in the Forefront of Racial Integration

Realizing that racial integration does not continue without positive intervention, the village pursued a variety of programs to promote and serve the community in a manner that attracts people of different races, ethnic groups, religious affiliations and economic means. These programs included affirmative marketing, Realtor education, housing counseling, and resident surveys. Shortly after becoming acting village manager, I executed and implemented an affirmative marketing agreement, a contract to assure that the listing agent marketed to majority group home seekers. This action triggered a nine year court action that ended in the United States Supreme Court. The Village ended up a clear winner in the courts.

Political Environment

One background element needs attention before I catalog the lessons learned from the Park Forest experience. Park Forest also had some idiosyncratic traditions related to elective office. First, the term of office for elected officials was two years until the late 1980s. This meant that elections were held every year, exposing the village board to turnover in half its members. Second, there was a tradition for everyone running on a non-partisan basis without affiliation and without any campaign collaboration. There was not a "group" that articulated a set of community expectations. These traditions apparently served the community well in its first three decades, especially when turnover exemplified by the "organization man" was commonplace—two good years of service was all that was reasonably expected. This elective process supported the tradition for extensive community deliberation, but was less inclined toward decisiveness.

Park Forest-Lessons Learned

Seek and Follow Good Leadership

The mayor is the key to manager support and success. The mayor is the key to the functioning of the governing body. How well he leads sets the tone for the organization and the community. I saw Bob Pierce follow this principle as I was learning. I now better understand why he did so. As Park Forest manager, I worked for two mayors who were very decent and I respected. One mayor had definitive ideas about what to accomplish and was comfortable advancing policies through the governing body. The other mayor, who initially took office as the interim mayor through a lottery, was not comfortable in managing conflict. He held the office of leader, but was besieged by three trustees who wanted to manipulate him, and all saw themselves as leaders. This situation was very debilitating to community building. Without effective mayoral leadership, the manager will not have an environment to help move the community forward. Eventually, the manager, who is responsible for getting results, will become a target for the ineffectiveness of the elected leadership.

Maximize Your Community Investment

The manager needs to do more than run an efficient service operation. He or she must help the community to invest wisely and optimize the investment to sustain the community into the future. You must facilitate the review of investment options by the board and staff. I was successful in the short term in Park Forest in making progress to build community. In hindsight, I should have tried to focus the community on long term realities for community building. Let me expand on some of those thoughts.

The manager must not lose sight of all the investment options that you have. I looked to investment in four areas: (1) housing; (2) infrastructure; (3) economic development; and (4) citizen participation. In Park Forest, it was the last of these investment paths—citizen participation or what I refer to later as citizen engagement--that was the option of least controversy and greatest potential. As I look back, and better understand the limitations of the situation, I would have devoted more attention to promoting citizen engagement. The investment choices for the community's future may have been more fruitful if we had been able to move citizen participation to citizen engagement.

Based upon my Woodridge education, I will talk more about moving citizen participation to citizen engagement. Citizen engagement is more attentive to establishing consensus or commitment to the mission and strategies necessary for moving the community forward. In the 1980s, Park Forest established the tagline "Capture the Spirit." We tried to do that, but more constructive citizen engagement—where all voices are heard and focused upon the mission--may have improved our investment performance. The Park Forest spirit certainly is the community's hallmark and the basis for its continuing success.

As I look back, I wish I had been more successful in engaging my board and the citizens around the reality of the future of Park Forest Plaza. We were very focused on "maintaining" the quality of community life and services. However, "maintenance" was not really an option. We were not able to engage around a future where the Park Forest Plaza was no longer a significant retail center.

My personal assessment of the dire future of the retail center, coupled with the unwillingness of the leadership team to engage around this issue, led me to believe that I would not be able to spend my entire career in Park Forest. I loved the "ideals and sacred things" for which this community stood, but I needed to face the reality that, if I was unable to move the community forward in its mission, I might not enjoy another seventeen years in Park Forest.

Developing Personal and Team Skills

There were many other important lessons that I learned in Park Forest before taking over as manager. Most of these lessons were about how not to develop a team. I noted that I worked for an "old school" manager. He was a traditional manager that believed in lines of authority and the role of support staff in day-to-day operations was limited. Thus, it was not a collegial environment where all opinions were solicited to formulate a "staff perspective."

The t-e-a-m in team is critical. Teamwork is essential to an organization that wants to be the best. The emphasis on "team" while I was an assistant was limited. Yet, I learned about how to fight for my perspective and persuade, convince, or ally with others in different ways. I also had opportunities that were not constrained by the organizational structure or limited by a directive boss. I was able to explore many areas for village improvement— labor relations, intergovernmental risk coverage, and diversity initiatives. Understand the limits and opportunities of any job that you choose and learn how to be constructive and successful in the environment in which you find yourself.

Communication is a basic part of team. A recurring theme amongst the younger generation of Park Forest professionals working under an "old school" manager was the inadequacy of "team" communications. This problem was rooted in the fact that we operated as a traditional bureaucratic hierarchy and there was not a commitment to "team." While we all contributed, we had limited interaction amongst the department managers and key staff. Staff meetings, formally or informally, were almost nonexistent. The team lacked synergy of a group. This operating environment regularly produced the confusion of "serial" communications. Serial communications is when operating information is passed along to one individual, then another, then another, and so on. When people don't convene as a group to make sure that they all have a common understanding and direction, then the group is less effective.

Stick with that which you enjoy. I stayed in Park Forest for eleven years before becoming the manager. I had opportunities to go elsewhere. Some of those opportunities would have been considered a "promotion." I stayed in Park Forest because I believed in the values of the community and I was doing challenging work, working with great people, and learning each day. Don't be in a rush to go elsewhere and move your career.

Service to community first. Communities benefit when managers and the staff make a long term commitment. Understanding the values of the community are so important to manager success, and that understanding is aided by tenure. Our profession needs to be builders of community first. Managers need to build the trust of the stakeholders in the community by showing absolute commitment to, and focus upon, the community. The job of a manager is not about career, but about community building.

Success of the manager depends upon understanding the community in a very intimate way. I have known professional colleagues who are very intent upon advancing their careers. They are intent upon replicating what they did in one town in a subsequent community, often times without assessing the situation or knowing the "fit" of the program with the community. These managers are dumbfounded when the program fails or meets with significant opposition.

Reality testing—know your limits. We all know that managers fail, or fall short of their own expectations. I make no judgments about those managers who find themselves in that unfortunate situation. On the contrary, I abhor "unhappy endings." I make this comment with the awareness of my own Park Forest experience. I was unable to help move the community forward in my last year. With the benefit of hindsight, I recognize that I did not sufficiently emphasize citizen engagement that helped to clarify the village mission and positive strategies to move forward. I needed to seek a "reality check" with the policy makers. I also recognize that there are limits to the ability of a manager to contribute to that process, because there are many other stakeholders who need to step up. This is another case of "Know thyself, know your limits." Be patient and take the time to develop a strategy that will allow you to build community.

Service and solace from team. The manager's job is often lonely. I learned in those early years that a regular source of support, energy, motivation and solace comes from the management team. Surround yourself with people committed to public service and develop the synergy of a group that helps build the community. Public service is important business. This group, more than any other, will help to carry on the "good fight."

The above lessons were valuable takeaways from my days in Park Forest. I didn't know the full measure of their value until I moved on to Woodridge.

Woodridge--Second Time Around
or Match Made In Heaven

We know that sometimes village boards are slow to act. Well, I might hold the record for a board taking its time to offer me the manager's job. I interviewed in Woodridge in early 1980. The Woodridge board offered me the job in 1989—about nine years later. I may be stretching it a bit. I interviewed for the Woodridge position in 1980 and 1988. The first time I interviewed I was not chosen. I consider myself fortunate to have stayed in Park Forest and learned more about success in city management. I now will provide some of the background for the community that, after a few months in my position, I often boasted that "I had died and gone to heaven."

Serving Post World War II Needs from Different Roots

Woodridge's beginnings reflected some of the same influences that existed in Park Forest. The economy of the post-World War II Chicago area, influenced by the returning veterans and the baby boom population explosion, eventually spread beyond Cook County and entered DuPage

County. Woodridge, however, did not have a master plan. Woodridge began as a simple subdivision.

Surety Builders, headed by Albert Kaufman, started Woodridge in 1958 by developing a plot of land southeast of 75th Street and Route 53. This development was on a ridge sloping toward the DuPage River near the 36 hole Woodridge Golf Course, thus inspiring the name "Woodridge." Veterans receiving loans insured through the GI Bill found Woodridge attractive, purchasing a majority of the homes. Like Park Forest, residents did not delay gathering together and voted overwhelmingly to incorporate in August 1959. The 109 home subdivision which encompassed less than a quarter of a square mile contained 459 people. Much like Park Forest, the early residents of Woodridge saw themselves as a community first and a subdivision second.

The entire area surrounding this first subdivision was covered by family farms and developers acquired these farms to construct homes and respond to the continuing strong demand in the housing market. The Winston Hills subdivision, developed by Winston-Muss Builders in 1964, significantly expanded Woodridge's land area to the north, and added about 5,000 to the Village's population. By the time of the 1970 census, Woodridge housed over 11,000 residents. The Woodridge Center development, annexed in 1972, doubled Woodridge's land area. The opening of Woodridge Drive in 1974 helped join the subdivisions via a convenient north-south thoroughfare, bearing the name of the community.

The growth of the 1970s was spurred by a significant number of multi-family units. This multi-family development of the 1970s satisfied some of the short term financial needs of the community. By 1980, the Village's population had grown to over 22,000. The recession of the early 80s slowed growth and fewer than five thousand residents were added by time of the next decennial census. By the time of the new millennium, Woodridge had reached 30,000. Although Woodridge, by most comparisons, was classified as a high growth community, its growth to 30,000 people took 30 years, about twenty years longer than Park Forest.

Woodridge Faces Challenges and Opportunities

I have already argued that it is necessary to see the unique character of each community. As a practicing local government professional, I now understand the benefit of having served in communities that in some respects are similar--and traced similar development paths. Even more beneficial from a professional development perspective is that I moved to a community that was tracing its path about twenty years later than the community that I had departed. As Woodridge hit the 30,000 population plateau, I was able to begin my work in Woodridge from a point in a community's history that I had already traced in Park Forest, and had the benefit of evaluating the outcome over a twenty year timeline. I've talked about some of the challenges that faced Park Forest after forty years. What deficiencies were exhibited in Woodridge in the late 1980s that presented challenges or needed to be addressed?

Higher Tax Rates. Woodridge's population and size mirrored that of Park Forest, both about five square miles and 30,000 people. Woodridge's combined property tax rate for the core of the community, the area covering school district 68 and Lisle-Woodridge fire district, was one of the highest in DuPage. Increasing costs for community services, especially schools, and rapid appreciation of real property values in combination sent tax rates and property tax bills higher in the late 1980s and early 1990s. Woodridge public officials realized that these high tax rates had to be addressed.

Need for Balanced Tax Base Growth. Woodridge, like Park Forest, had developed as a starter home community for GIs. The housing was functional and affordable. Woodridge also built a substantial supply of multi-family housing during the 1970s. The combination of affordable single family and basic garden-style apartments meant that the tax base per capita was also lower than most DuPage communities. This low per capita tax base largely explains the high total property tax rate.

Beginning in the early 1980s, Woodridge public officials, led by the new mayor William Murphy, placed emphasis upon changing the type of development and the net value of new development. The board had barred approval of any new multi-family units. We will see later how key stakeholders in the community worked to address these deficiencies in the value of the tax base and the character and type of development, pursuing balanced growth.

Growth Now or Never. Woodridge confirmed in the adoption of its 1985 Comprehensive Plan the need to change those elements of its plan for development that would threaten its ability to be a successful over the long term. Woodridge also recognized that it was still subject to changes in its environment. The Illinois State Toll Highway Authority, as the 1980s unfolded, was progressing with construction of a road bisecting Woodridge and connecting Interstate 88 with Interstate 55. This road would provide pressure for development and competition for annexations amongst communities in its path. Thus, in the late 1980s, Woodridge was faced with the challenge to take advantage of opportunities for change.

Finding a Good Administrator. Perhaps the biggest challenge that faced Woodridge in the late 1980s was the need for stable, effective managerial leadership. The village had four "permanent" administrators and two one-year stints under an acting administrator in the ten years before my arrival. This history of turnover on the surface does not speak positively to the prospect for managerial longevity. However, my contact with the mayor both during my 1980 interview (he was a trustee at the time) and the 1989 selection process suggested that this was an eminently capable individual—and "good person." He was respected by everyone with whom I spoke. The elected official team worked together effectively.

The basic philosophy of how the organization operated--respect for roles, involvement of staff in key decisions, an emphasis on professional performance, board members doing their homework and expecting the same from staff, a series of employee and community recognition programs, and well-structured land and financial planning processes—all were more than I expected. All these elements were tributes to the elected leadership that selected me, and to whom I am so grateful for the opportunity. All I had to do in Woodridge was provide the effective professional management component.

CHAPTER 3

LEADER VALUES—VALUED LEADERSHIP

The city is sacred. This is the quintessence of our profession. I know that this is a dramatic claim, but it is part of how I need to explain my own experiences. Those who have practiced in the city management profession for any length of time will understand if there is a key to success that it is all about values. The principle of value-based leadership may be as difficult to describe as it is to practice. Value-based leadership works when it is supported and reinforced. It is magnified when it starts from a strong foundation of public leadership. I will articulate what I see as those values, what support is necessary, and how they can lead to success in a career and for the communities which you manage. In the first part of this chapter, I will describe the basic values that the manager must have to perform successfully. The second part of this chapter will highlight the personal characteristics and management philosophy that support success.

Day One—Career Choice Confirmed

My first day on the job as a full time professional was January 31, 1972. As assistant to the manager, I was assigned the task of drafting the annual report of the mayor. I reviewed the files for the prior reports and I was intrigued, maybe awed is a better description, by the final paragraph in the 1970 report of B.G. "Barney" Cunningham. He quoted the Oath of the Athenian City State:

We will never bring disgrace on this our City by an act of dishonesty or cowardice. We will fight for the ideals and Sacred Things of the City both alone and with many. We will revere and obey the City's laws, and will do our best to incite a reverence and respect in those above us who are prone to annul them or set them at naught. We will strive increasingly to quicken the public's sense of civic duty. Thus in all these ways we will transmit this City, not only not less, but greater and more beautiful than it was transmitted to us.

This oath so reflected my motivation for entering the city management profession. The oath reflected my dreams for the work that I was beginning. In looking back, I'm inclined to interpret this first day experience as unfolding under a "guiding hand" or blessings from above. While I was a fan of Aristotle from college (a University of Chicago thing) and the oath graced the wall of the Maxwell School lobby, I had not previously seen this oath. It captured my motivation for seeking a career in public service. Literally starting day one, I found my career choice reinforced and I was captivated with trying to fulfill this oath. Given my competitiveness, this oath also provided legitimacy to my nature to "fight the good fight."

Community is Special, Sacred

People who come together to live in a community have many reasons— shelter, job, education, family roots, and many other reasons. Professional city managers need to see their city as special, if not sacred. When people come together, they are counting on that community to meet their basic needs. Many of them are looking to the community for more than the basic life necessities. They want their children to enjoy sports, to learn, and to find a place near mom and dad to live when they grow up. Residents want to be free from the threat of crime, walk in the park, or bike to the town centre. Communities provide residents with an intimacy that nurtures the family unit and the potential for each person to develop. Professional managers need to embrace the importance that people place on their city. It has to be as important to the city manager. The city manager has to prove that he will embrace the sacred things of the city.

Trust and Faith

In my final "Message from the Administrator" in the Woodridge employee newsletter, I said that I needed to explain the importance of trust and faith "amongst the people who reinforced it and made it a basic rule for how I live." I consider these twin values as basic to public service. If the work we do is important, in fact sacred, we need to be believers in the basic goodness of the people in our community. If we don't believe and embrace that basic goodness, then we can't pursue the "ideals" of the city in the Athenian Oath. These twin values have many perspectives from which to be viewed, upon which I will expand.

Trust and faith begins from within and is learned and acquired as one grows up. Belief in ones own goodness is essential to having trust and faith in others. The manager needs to have trust and faith in order to take ownership for his actions. This basic value will help convey the passion and importance of the work to those surrounding the manager.

Trust and faith extends in many other directions. Each day we need to convey the importance of our work, especially to employees, through whom we work to care for the needs of the community. We need to believe that they have a similar view of the community and have the same trust and faith in their work efforts. We need to put our trust and faith in those employees, and their commitment to this important work as well as their ability to make outstanding contributions to the community. As I noted in that final employee newsletter, "my trust and faith in others has been paid back tenfold and invariably returned by the recipient."

As a professional manager, working for a community and its diverse set of stakeholder interests, you can best multiply your impact by having trust and faith in the people implementing the community's work. I have always been inclined to see people as a Type Y personality rather than a Type X—people put effort forward for work that they enjoy and are permitted the ingenuity and creativity to succeed.

The manager is doing this important community work through the trust and faith that the community has placed in the manager through the elected officials. The trust and faith that the mayor and board placed in me was extended through the organization and community. I was just reflecting the twin values of trust and faith for which I was the conservator or guardian. As long as a manager is entrusted with responsibility, and continues to maintain that trust and faith, the manager can work to meet the noblest aspirations of the community.

Our professional education programs have often focused on the need for servant leadership as a basic approach to managing our organizations. Servant leadership as summarized by Spears in the Non-profit Reader On Leadership is based on "teamwork and community...involves others in decision making...ethical and caring behavior...enhances the personal growth of people." I would summarize Spears behaviors for servant leadership simply—have trust and faith in those around you!

The times in my career when I felt in greatest jeopardy of losing my job were situations that involved a loss of trust with one or more board members. In those situations, I was fortunate to have supporters and counselors who coached me as to how to rebuild that trust. These situations helped teach me that maintaining trust and faith was essential.

In *Learning to Lead*, Warren Bennis and Joan Goldsmith talk about trust being the linchpin of leadership. A leader who establishes trust will marshal individuals to contribute to the group. Goldsmith and Bennis simply state that "trust is the key ability that inspires those who join them to create movements for social change and build organizations to realize their dreams." They add, "Trust provides the motivation and energy that makes it possible for organizations to be successful."

Integrity

Integrity is the first pledge in the Athenian Oath and it is at the heart of the Code of Ethics of the International City/County Management Association (ICMA). Integrity and honesty are essential to a manager's success. When elected officials lose trust and faith in the manager, you can usually look to a perceived lack of truthfulness or honesty. Integrity is the glue that helps to maintain the trust and faith of the elected officials.

We know that acting with integrity is much more difficult than preaching about it. Integrity means painstakingly fulfilling commitments. Integrity occurs when you give the benefit of the doubt to those to whom you made a commitment even when they fall short. Integrity means letting people know what to expect from you. Perhaps the greatest practical difficulty for practicing integrity in the local government setting is the ability to articulate policy choices clearly and without manipulation.

Respect

A basic value that flows from all those already put forth is respect for the people, places, institutions, and groups with whom you work. Working in building community means respecting the aspirations of all its stakeholders. The "sacred things" of the city require that we show respect. This notion of inclusion and service for all people is also a tenet of the ICMA Code. We will talk in the remaining chapters how we build on this basic value to connect all the people in building community.

It All Starts at the Top

I promised to share some of the principles to successful management. I like to "boil down" these principles. It all starts with the mayor! Value-based leadership works, and is sustained, when it is supported and reinforced. There is no better "reinforcer" in the city organization than the mayor. He leads the governance team. He seeks to get the "right people on the bus." I had the good fortune of working my last twenty years with a mayor that fits the Level 5 leader designation of Jim Collins. He possesses the combination of "deep personal humility with intense professional will." At my retirement reception, I saluted Mayor Murphy as my "soul mate in good governance." During that reception, the mayor and staff described a number of personal qualities that I possessed. I was fortunate that the mayor's values and leadership style mirrored and complemented my own.

The personal qualities and leadership qualities that we shared included:

- Inclusion—lead and develop all stakeholders
- Challenge all to do their best
- Empower others to succeed
- Work from strengths
- Be a caring mentor to improve people
- Encourage creativity

- Stick to the mission
- Respect everyone's role
- Be tenacious and persevering in pursuit of your objective
- Regularly collect data and benchmark
- Appreciate and recognize those around you
- Make decisions with emotional intelligence
- Be genuine; be yourself
- Make work fun

Bennis and Goldsmith in *Learning to Lead* share four characteristics that a leader possesses to establish "followership"—vision, integrity, empathy, and commitment. I was fortunate to work with a mayor that epitomized these characteristics. The mayor and I started with a good relationship and improved upon it each day. He was a very hard worker and appreciated the same in those in whom he had placed his trust. I worked hard to build upon that trust and fulfill his expectations. In return, I received his support even during significant conflicts—internally and externally

Partnerships Based Upon Routine Communication

The mayor practiced many routines to manage his own busy schedule and fulfill all his commitments. One of his routines was in meeting with me each week for an hour. We communicated in other ways, but this was an important routine. The mayor came to each meeting with his list—and I came with mine. We discussed what was on the agenda, feedback from community members, policy issues and processes, and anything else that was important to moving the community forward. Whenever we needed to add a meeting to the schedule, or add someone to the conversation, the mayor was willing to help if I asked. The support was reciprocal.

The weekly meeting with the mayor that sticks in my mind most was back in summer 1991. This event epitomizes how well we worked together as partners and reinforced our best characteristics. Woodridge had recently experienced a couple high profile police incidents in one of the multi-family neighborhoods. The treatment of the incidents by the press was worse than our perception of reality. As the old saying goes, perception is reality, which routinely applies in a community if you do not address the matter.

At our weekly meeting after these incidents, the mayor and I quickly took up the subject. I am not sure which of us initiated the subject, but our agreement on the situation and what should be done to address it was speedy. We could neither ignore the reality nor perception. It must be addressed. This was an opportunity. The more publicly that we address the situation, the stronger will be the commitment from stakeholders to address any issues identified. We had already started major code enforcement measures in this neighborhood and we could build on that impetus to make even more significant improvements.

Task Force for a Quality Community

How did we follow-up on this meeting and these important conclusions? We established a task force—The Quality Community Task Force. The Task Force was charged with identifying what the community could do to address the perceptions of this incident and what other steps could be taken in the areas of policing, housing, youth, and diversity. What does the community do well? How can Woodridge improve? The Task Force was not intended to be a feint. It was expected to produce positive results—another vehicle to engage residents. The mayor appointed (1) key stakeholders from other governmental bodies, (2) citizens reflecting the community's diversity who had an interest in improving the community and a record for action, and (3) the village administrator, police chief, and building and zoning director.

The Task Force proved to be a pivotal point in engaging the community for improvement. The Task Force is best known for its support of the multi-family license ordinance, which was approved in December 1993. The multi-family license ordinance, more than any other programmatic initiative, provided support and leverage for a major reinvestment in Woodridge multi-family housing, and significantly added to the economic base of the community.

The Quality Community Task Force was linked to other citizen engagement efforts to improve the targeted neighborhood through engagement of residents in the community. The Community Resource Center, a neighborhood after-school facility, gained support for community policing and bringing together community volunteers to encourage youth in the community. The Park District undertook significant steps to redevelop area parks based upon task force recommendations. Echo Point Park bordered the neighborhood and was overgrown and underused. Based upon task force input, this park was transformed and became home to the annual all village garage sale. This task force process was an important experience and success in building the citizen engagement process discussed in chapter 5. The chair of the Task Force became so engaged that we did an extensive assessment of our civic infrastructure, using the National Civic League civic index, and applied for the All-America City award. We all learned how to improve engagement of the community.

The Quality Community Task Force boosted my partnership with the mayor and board. The community leadership team, with excellent staff support, tackled an important issue in the community by engaging all the players. We directly faced all conflicts and issues. Our only "spin" was how we can improve the neighborhood and the community. My weekly meeting with the mayor helped build a platform and capacity for addressing many other community issues.

Sign of the Times

There were some other memorable moments from those meetings with the mayor. We gained one of the Woodridge's largest employers through our teamwork. Back in 1999, the board gave us some parameters by which to attract the Morey Corporation to Woodridge. The mayor and I met with key corporate officers and explained how we could assist. The Morey representative liked the site in Woodridge, but expressed concern about the company's relationship with local government.

Morey wanted a community that would be a solid partner and deliver on its promises. The Morey officer wanted to have a "presence" in Woodridge. He may have mentioned the value of having a vanity address. I do remember the mayor and me talking immediately after the meeting. We agreed that we had to send a message about the relationship that we wanted to build with these people. I do believe that he was reading my mind when he asked "can we name a street for them?" I said that I would check on that possibility for the location proposed.

I checked with the public works director. He confirmed that we could name that street "Morey Boulevard" and he offered to have a sign produced with that name. The decision was going to be finalized the next morning. Shortly before the Morey officers gathered for that decision meeting, the mayor and I delivered to the Morey Corporation the Morey Boulevard sign. We later learned that the decision was favorable and, if there was any doubt, the sign was a symbol that sealed the deal. Woodridge has enjoyed an outstanding relationship with Morey ever since—and the company has added to its headquarters twice.

Curiosity Killed the Cat—Lack of it Fired the Manager

I acquired, or at the very least refined, one important management quality as a result of these meetings with the mayor. Whenever he posed a question that I could not answer, I learned that I needed to learn the answer as well as understand why he posed the question. I found that when the mayor asked a question that he was "exploring." Since I have a similar proclivity, I began to better understand the importance of curiosity. I also learned that curiosity could aid my relationships with most everyone around me. Be slower to reach conclusions and try to understand the question, the questioner, and how you can help with your answer. This became an important tool in the kit as I moved forward in Woodridge. Curiosity may be the most helpful measure to repair and maintain the twin values of trust and faith—the foundation for building all your relationships. Failure to maintain curiosity is often related to the downfall of the manager.

!#+ Happens

Building a partnership with the mayor and board can be an important protection when difficult moments arise. We all have experiences that are embarrassing, and my early efforts to cement these partnerships in Woodridge quickly paid dividends. One of my early "battles" with DuPage County was over the odor generated at the sewer treatment plant. I lived in the neighborhood of the facility. I was alerted to the odor problem when one of my neighbors knocked on my door and asked me to step outside-- and smell. There was some evidence "in the air." He explained that a group of residents had formed an odor task force to monitor how the county was remedying the problem.

I learned more about this problem through village staff and attending related meetings at the county. There was agreement that "things were not right." As with other problems described in the course of this book, I learned about what was happening by visiting the site and "wandered around." I had visited several times and photographed several of the sludge disposal practices that contributed to the excess odor. On my last unofficial tour with my camera and seven year old son in hand, I tried to exit and found the site gate closed. I made contact with the plant manager who assisted with my exit. The plant manager must have mentioned my visit to the responsible county board member.

The following day I woke up to find an article in the Chicago Tribune explaining how the Woodridge mayor and board had been notified in writing by the county board chair that the village administrator had been trespassing on the site. The county required the village and its administrator in the future to obtain formal permission before entering the site. Well, I had some explaining to do--and I did. I was not excited by the notoriety. There was some uneasiness on my part and the board. The mayor responded that the village and its administrator would follow appropriate procedures for access. The mayor "pulled me out of it." As time passed, the village became more engaged with the citizen odor task force and worked to remedy the plant operating issues. Although there were some tense moments early on from my "high profile" involvement in this issue, I was able to eventually show that I was "fighting for the ideals of the city."

CHAPTER 4

LEADERSHIP TEAM UNIFIED FOR SUCCESS

Connecting Groups is Key to Community Building

Communities are built by bringing people together in a constructive synergy. The manager needs to act as a "connector" who facilitates bringing these people together; the larger the group, the louder the chorus. Remember—effective local government is all about making connections and using them to build community.

If you want everyone to participate, which groups are critical? There are three groups around which you need to build effective relationships and upon which you will rely if you are going to add to the community chorus. The first group is the elected officials—the mayor and trustees. The second group is the management team—department managers and key professionals who you rely upon for carrying out day-to-day operations. The third group is the citizens and other stakeholders (businesses, realtors, taxing bodies, etc.) who influence the success of the community.

In this chapter I will focus upon how the manager needs to connect to the elected officials. The greater the unity of this leadership team of elected officials and manager, the more success that the community will experience in fulfilling its mission. In later chapters, we will address citizen/stakeholder connections and marshalling the best efforts of the management team.

Mayor and Manager--Partners for Building Board Continuity and Capacity

The mayor is key to your success. The mayor is leader of the board. The mayor is leader of the community. If you help the mayor lead, you will likely succeed. If you think that it is his job alone, you will do both yourself and the mayor a disservice, and diminish the possibility for outstanding results.

Jim Banovetz, architect of the fine public administration program at Northern Illinois University, most accurately described the ideal relationship between mayor and manager as a partnership. I know that I could not have had the success and enjoyment in Woodridge without the partnership that I had with the mayor.

Managers should not see their role as leading the board. The manager's role is simplified if you see the mayor as leading the board and the manager as serving the mayor and board. What did the mayor do in Woodridge to help form the elected official team and establish his leadership role? What was the socialization process for trustees and their role in governance of the community? How new elected officials are incorporated into the governance team is important for the manager to understand and support.

"Drafting" Trustees to Join the Team

The first step in the socialization process starts before the trustee gains a seat on the board; it starts with how new members are brought onto the board and encouraged to become an elected official. Managers are keenly aware of the value of stable leadership and the benefits of continuity in the governing body. The process for accomplishing this continuity was much different in Woodridge than Park Forest. My view is that the Woodridge experience has yielded greater success in terms of stable, continuous governance. Park Forest had both a non-partisan and independent tradition for municipal elections. There were no teams, slates, or "affiliated" candidates in Park Forest. All candidates were independents. The probability of a "one-issue" candidate being elected in Park Forest was much higher. This presented a greater challenge for continuity of board leadership.

Because of this "less-connected" leadership environment in Park Forest, I began the orientation process before the election—in an effort to build the sense of a leadership team as soon as possible. I would hold a Saturday morning forum for candidates after petitions had been filed but before the campaign began. We introduced all the department managers who had an opportunity to share information on their operations and the issues that faced the village in the year ahead. We responded to questions and spelled out how we would respond to questions during the campaign. The greater stability in the Woodridge elected leadership permitted me to be less "upfront" in the trustee orientation process in Woodridge and defer to the mayor. Trustees in Woodridge generally came into office with a broad commitment to the methods and values that had been practiced.

The Woodridge mayor is now in his eighth term. Despite the mayor's longevity, I saw considerable change in the group of trustees who served during my twenty years as administrator, but a simultaneous steadiness—continuity—in how the group approached their role. The mayor was chiefly responsible for both continuity of the governing body and accommodating change. The mayor sought to add members to the board that evidenced support for the values of the community and the goals that had been established through the strategic management process. He sought new board members based upon how individuals would enhance the ability of the board to govern—intellectual capacity, commitment to the community, and diversity reflective of the community.

The socialization process continued after election to office. Before the new trustee had his or her first official board meeting, the mayor sat down with the newly elected trustee for an orientation. The mayor's orientation addresses trustee role and responsibilities, including various meetings and their purpose in reaching board policies, communication tools like the administrator memorandum, and the strategic management process. The new trustee also learns about the role of the administrator covering duties spelled out under the code of ordinances, the process for evaluating the administrator, and the employment agreement. The mayor's trustee orientation also includes information on the village code, intergovernmental organizations, legal counsel, comprehensive plan, and important annual meetings.

During the many trustee changes that I encountered, I was impressed by how the mayor mentored each one of these trustees—there were no "outsiders"—all were treated with respect. He was patient. He was sensitive to their struggles with difficult decisions. He also empowered each trustee. He expected that each trustee would do the homework to make a decision. He didn't consider it necessary to "tell" them how to vote. I was surprised on how few issues he tried to change their mind. The mayor "picked his fights." If the mayor saw the issue as critical to village direction, he did extra homework and provided thoughtful, constructive comments.

The trustees who worked with the mayor had respect for his leadership and the way they were treated. Under this leadership, the governing body flourished despite the changes in elected officials. The public meetings chaired by the mayor branded the community as a bastion of decorum and respect.

Manager is Numero Uno Board Resource

The mayor communicates the basic measures as leader of the governing body to orient, acclimate, and educate the newly elected official to life as a trustee. The administrator next works to build on the orientation work of the mayor; my objective was initially to add to the new trustee's understanding of issues that would soon face the board, particularly in the next agenda or two. All elected officials want to be good policy-makers. Managers need to understand this and, despite differences in decision-making style of board members, need to find how to be responsive and be the number one resource for each elected official—and for the mayor and board collectively.

New trustees (and those with more experience) were encouraged to (1) ask questions; (2) ask questions early; (3) ask as many questions as necessary; (4) ask questions from whatever source and however triggered; and (5) ask questions big and small—all are important; there are only "gold stars" for asking, no demerits. The administrator, with whatever staff or professional resources required, will provide answers to the questions. I became even more convinced of this "ask-ask-ask" philosophy toward the end of my tenure in Woodridge because I had three new Board members at the same time. While I always worked hard to anticipate the needs for background information, I was never absolutely sure about the trustees' level of understanding. I relished getting questions—because I knew that the trustee was digesting the information. The question also helped me to understand in what ways I needed to further the trustee education process.

Understanding Roles for Effective Decision Making

One of these new Woodridge trustees was struggling with difficult policy issues related to the economic downturn of 2008-09 as we finalized basic decisions related to trimming the 2009-10 budget. Of course, we were all struggling, board and staff alike. The decisions that faced Woodridge and every other community were unprecedented in my thirty-eight years of shaping budgets. This trustee was concerned about the compensation adjustments that we were considering in executive session. Given the difficulty of the decision, I was never more gratified by the way board and staff worked toward a final decision. I must highlight some of the elements of that decision making process that aided an outcome that was supported by the group.

First, the staff understood that the choice was a policy decision of the board and the board needed to "own it." We did not want to rush the board to make a choice unless it was prepared to stick with the policy. I learned as my career progressed that if time assisted the board in coming to a group decision then give the board more time, and provide whatever additional information that was needed to reach a sound judgment. As the discussion of compensation policy progressed over about a month's time, I was able to highlight that the perspectives of department managers mirrored the struggles of various board members.

Second, the discussion revealed that some board members were not comfortable with the option preferred by the staff. The trustee noted above asked for several "more" choices calculating outcomes. I encouraged him to translate his concerns into what he considered to be the values that the community would expect us to live by in the difficult economy. Rather than "back into" a number, I encouraged this trustee to share with the board and staff what he thought would maintain our credibility with the community. The staff would translate the value desired by the board into one or more options for implementation with employees. The assistant administrator greatly aided this discussion by preparing a summary of values and priorities embodied in our compensation policy, helping to focus the decision on values and policy.

Third, the mayor, who had previously indicated his support for one option, shared that he had concerns as well and, based upon values voiced by the trustees, would support another option. He voiced his support for coming to a conclusion that all elected officials could publicly support. His leadership finally produced a narrow range of options that the board discussed in terms of financial responsibility, employee support, and compassion for residents hit by economic conditions. We arrived at a point of agreement that all board members embraced. The mayor and I expressed admiration and appreciation for the process that the board and staff had navigated to reach a conclusion. We were all proud of the work of the group.

The trustee who had been struggling to be comfortable with his decision by doing his own calculation of different outcomes came up to me two weeks later. He said that he now appreciated the encouragement to reach a value judgment and the staff would work to give the board good options—whatever the path. He found the process helpful to his decision making role.

Good Data Make Good Decisions

Managers see themselves as the professional—"the expert." That is why a community employs a professional. The Woodridge mayor tells local government groups in Illinois that the "administrator is expected to make recommendations, to take issues however complex, and provide an appropriate overview, summary of the disadvantages and advantages of various options and recommendations." The manager needs to make sure that issues are properly dissected and analyzed and complexities understood. Within that context, the manager needs to develop data that aids the understanding of his board members. Board members can only make good decisions with good data. Serving this need of board members is near the top of the list of duties for any professional.

Understanding the mentality of a manager, I am reasonably sure that you are now asking what is "good data?" I know that's what you are thinking. In most situations, I believe that I could answer this question with reasonable certainty. The difficulty is in combining the situational analytical dictates with the decision making styles of each board member and the board collectively. My description sounds complex—and sometimes it is. The remainder of this chapter and the next will provide examples of sorting through the data and analyzing it. A clear mission and following the components of the strategic management process helps a manager identify options and the analysis related thereto.

Good Data for Senior Housing

Let me illustrate the value of how "good data" helps to make good decisions—especially for the purpose of aiding the development of the manager's relationship with the board. This example is the formulation of a senior housing policy and action plan for Woodridge.

The planning and development department routinely provides demographic data to the board and other stakeholders, depending upon the needs of the interested party. The department has noted on many occasions that the village is somewhat "younger" than an average community. Woodridge also has limited supply of housing especially designed for seniors.

About 2005, the feedback at the annual town meeting increasingly voiced concern for, and interest in, providing for senior needs, including housing. This community "voice" became clearer with each subsequent town meeting. The board and staff recognized the need to anticipate, and begin planning for, this expressed community need. Concurrently, the board was exploring with staff a redevelopment of a mid-size apartment complex. Redevelopment of the apartment complex was expected to dramatically increase the property tax generated at this site—a key element of investment for sustainable development. This project also met the village's goal of balanced development. Board and staff studied this development project for about two years. A plan and development agreement with the owner was eventually reached. The village agreed to acquire part of the parcel for senior housing development.

More Prep Means Less Blood on the Battlefield

The director of planning and development subscribes to one of my axioms learned from the basic training drill sergeant at Fort Jackson—"more prep means less blood on the battlefield." Do all the work needed before pushing for a decision on the issue. Having a site for "senior housing" still leaves many questions unanswered. What are the real needs? How can they be addressed?

The board and staff agreed to a process to obtain "good data" so that a "good decision" could be achieved. First step in the process was to review demographic data from a well-regarded analyst, including how the community's available housing matched up with future senior needs. Second, village staff reviewed how the redevelopment site, as well as other parcels in Woodridge, matched up with the projected future needs.

Staff also mapped out all the available senior housing in the immediate Woodridge market area. The results of these analyses were shared with the board. It was an effective educational process for everyone. The board gave an indication of future preferences for development of the sites studied and the board identified yet more questions that would be helpful in the process of reaching specific guidelines for the apartment complex redevelopment site.

Third step in the process was to tour a range of senior housing developments so that types of facilities, financing, and amenities could be better understood by the board and staff. The fourth phase of the process was to hold a community forum to gain more input from residents as to how their needs might be addressed by senior housing at the redevelopment site. The board and staff are currently preparing to take all this information and send out a request for qualifications to solicit developers who can meet the identified needs.

Connections to the Community

This senior housing example shows how the board, manager, staff, and citizens stay connected in making important community decisions. You start with input from residents, gain general direction from the board, and work with staff to support understanding the issue to develop a final action plan. The board can deliberately map out what questions need to be addressed to reach a decision that fulfills the community's mission. Because the process anticipates future community needs and action steps, the board can anticipate each step that it will take with the confidence that it is participating in an effective process. The process is iterative, providing feedback to board, staff, and citizens as progress occurs. We will soon turn to how the strategic management process engages citizens, and provides everyone the opportunity to develop trust and faith in the pursuit of the "ideals and sacred things" of the city. Before we turn to citizen engagement, however, I want to complete my comments on how the board and manager stay connected.

Equitable Sharing of Information Builds Trust

A rule near the top of a manager's list for providing information to elected officials is to share the information with them all. This rule provides many benefits. First, the manager needs to avoid playing favorites. Most board members will accept this rule as one measure of fairness and equal treatment. The last thing that a manager wants at a board meeting is for a trustee to dispute an argument of another board member by saying, "you probably aren't aware, but the manager told me this when he shared this other information." Second, board members benefit from understanding the issues. Information requests, and the corresponding response from the manager, help to educate the elected official. Third, sharing information with all elected officials, and doing it well before the board's final decision, permits all the questions and concerns to surface before that final decision. I have regularly seen this "lead up" to a tough or complex policy decision help board and staff understands options or analysis that best serve all competing perspectives.

Communication does not just happen. It needs to be structured, timely, and provide "good data." Two important communication opportunities with the board are the weekly manager's report to the board and the board's evaluation of the manager. The administrator's memorandum (AM) was a weekly tradition in Woodridge well before my time. However, it did not appear to have a clear purpose. The AM of the 80s was usually an assemblage of articles or reports from other government entities and often contained long reports without any staff analysis or perspective on how the information integrates with the village's operational responsibilities.

The AM of the 80s was a report of the administrator to the board— neither owned by nor a responsibility of the department manager. The AM was not an integration of all the operating departments of the village. When I began the weekly manager's report in Park Forest, I asked the department managers to tell the story about the weekly progress on important projects. Good things were being done---and we needed to tell people, especially the board. The <u>management team</u> needed to be responsible for this weekly update.

The first change that I asked Woodridge department managers to make in the AM was to become the reporters for this weekly "news magazine." The AM has become a weekly update for the board on routine operational data, progress on projects, meeting calendar, feedback from citizens of a positive or negative nature, "heads up" issues, and issues that have arisen in other communities. The AM is also used to provide background to the board on upcoming issues for which the administrator is seeking board feedback before placing the matter on the board agenda for final action.

The AM, along with the feedback process already described, was a way to educate the board and allow them to anticipate issues which they would eventually face. The board was constantly "in the loop" through the sharing of weekly data. We often tried to identify the timeline for when the board would use the information that we shared.

Do Not Miss the Evaluation

The second "must have" communication tool for the manager is the annual evaluation. This is also an important policy making choice for the board. The evaluation of a manager is probably the second most important decision of the board—second only to hiring the manager. The expectation for an annual evaluation should be spelled out in the manager's first contract. It is best to start evaluations at the beginning of a manager's tenure, not after a dispute has arisen and the board needs to "take the manager to the woodshed." It is from this vantage point that I have frequently heard managers refer to the evaluation as "painful." I had the experience myself in Park Forest. Routine evaluations were abandoned in Park Forest when the mayor who was elected was conflict averse. The avoidance of conflict increased the frustration of everyone involved. This is another reason that I suggest looking to the mayor's leadership.

When you have a good mayor, work with him or her to design and support the evaluation process. The Woodridge mayor spoke to ICMA members about evaluation at the 1994 Chicago conference. He emphasized that to foster the productivity and performance of the administrator that an evaluation process must be in place. He also believes strongly that the evaluation tool should provide the administrator with a general overview of the manager's performance but also a process that identifies how <u>each</u> elected official views the administrator's performance.

I was part of this process for twenty years. I have every reason to support this advice. If the manager encounters conflict with one or more board members, this evaluation tool is an excellent structure from which to identify the concerns and begin to address them. If you avoid addressing whatever concerns that exist with board members, you increase the chance that you will lose the opportunity to mend the relationship.

Do not miss your opportunity to evaluate the board! Evaluation is a two-way street. The evaluation process is a good opportunity for you to give the board some feedback. At every evaluation, I would remind the board of the importance of clear direction from them. I would point to specific examples of serving our mission more effectively because of that clear direction from the board. From time-to-time, the evaluation process and instrument was supplemented by other tools such as the ICMA 360 degree evaluation used for Credentialed Managers. The Credential Manager, and the underlying skill set, is an excellent way to educate the board on what a manager and his staff must do to be high quality professionals.

The manager builds a sound relationship with the board through his partnership with the mayor. He sustains and enhances that relationship with the board by being a top notch policy making resource and maintaining close communication on an ongoing basis—giving the board a window to the community. This close relationship with the board puts the board and the staff in a unified position to take on the challenge of engaging citizens to build community which we will explore in the next chapter.

CHAPTER 5

ENGAGING CITIZENS IN BUILDING A FIRST CLASS COMMUNITY

Citizen Engagement—Mission Impossible?

Your assignment, if you choose to accept it, is to connect 35,000 plus residents to their government--to join in building the community. This is the challenge to become a successful manager. Citizens are the second group with which the manager must build a relationship—play the role of "connector."

Perhaps the relationship that is central to managers, in fact the very concept of public, is the relationship between the citizen and the professional. We know that there are many approaches to how the interactions amongst the elected officials, manager and citizen may occur, be shared, and be managed.

First, I will explain several elements of the citizen engagement process that arose from early strategic planning efforts in Woodridge. Woodridge now calls the entire process—strategic management—after years of fine tuning. The board has used the current form of the strategic management process since the late 1990s. I will provide a complete overview of strategic management in the Strategies for Building Community chapter.

Second, I will introduce below the basic community citizen engagement elements that encouraged all stakeholders to participate. I will then outline two components of how we worked with employees to geometrically increase our impact. One component revolves around what we did to motivate employees to strive for "superior service" and to improve the "quality of life" which are both factors central to the village mission. The other component is about how we provided support to employees to accomplish the citizen engagement/service task.

Building Community from the Outside In

Without engaging your residents and stakeholders in the purpose or mission of the community, you can't build community. How do you engage the resident in shaping and fulfilling this mission? In Woodridge, we built our strategic management process around several events or processes that relied upon citizen involvement and input. Community involvement, more importantly citizen engagement, is at the core of the annual strategic process—the core of how decisions are made. Three primary avenues exist for citizen engagement—(1) the community needs survey (CNS); (2) town meeting; and (3) neighborhood dialogues.

Community Needs Survey—Trends for 25 Years

Woodridge has conducted a community needs survey possibly longer than any community in the country. This survey has been regularly performed for twenty-five years—another valuable building block in place when I arrived in Woodridge. The community needs survey (CNS) provides a baseline assessment of what residents think about the quality of community and the performance of village services. This survey of about fifty questions is randomly sent to 1200 households, with an option for online completion. Response rates have ranged between 35 and 45 percent. Considerable effort is put into insuring that all segments (single family, multi-family, and condos) of the community are included in the survey. Parts of the survey are designed to elicit concerns from residents or obtain new ideas.

I can attest to the volume of comments that residents take time to share. It becomes very clear that they wish to contribute to the direction of the community, and they take seriously how the village incorporates their input into community betterment. One resident aptly characterized how he expected the input to be used, "I think that the village has done a great job, but we must always be looking for ways to make things better for as many facets of the residents as possible. Keep up the good work!"

The CNS, as the historic baseline for citizen evaluation, is the key benchmark for assessing improvements in the quality of life and service performance. The results of CNS are also shared widely with citizens and employees. These results become a measure for all to use—as an improvement tool and a mark of success. The mayor and board incorporate this feedback into the annual goal setting process

Town Meeting

Woodridge holds a town meeting annually. This meeting is the largest gathering each year for citizen participation, and engages citizens on important issues which face the community in the coming year, and on a long term basis. The Village advertises the meeting broadly and sends out 600 invitations requesting attendance. Woodridge emphasizes participation by a group that is reflective of the entire population, which is quite diverse.

The town meeting, usually numbering 200 participants, kicks off with a light supper for the attendees. The town meeting is a social event, permitting old and new acquaintances to be formed and promoting the neighborly character of community governance. The town meeting "business" format has three components. First, the mayor reports on significant community mileposts since the last gathering. Background is provided on important community issues, including pertinent data produced through the CNS. The second part of the meeting is a face-to-face facilitated conversation. Staff members and trustees serve as facilitators in round table discussions, each containing 10-15 persons, addressing questions that help guide the Village in the coming years. The third part of the evening concludes with residents prioritizing ideas and issues that are important to them and the village at large. Priorities are then aggregated in a document and utilized for the next phases of the annual strategic management process—goal setting and budget.

When you have a large community meeting like the town meeting, you always have concerns about the "unknown." What if an individual or group attempts to "hijack" the meeting for their own purpose? It is not unusual to encounter such behavior. We have individuals each year who have their issues for airing. The small group discussion format, along with some "policing" by their neighbors at the table, reduces the impact of individual disruptive behavior. Before we expanded the town meeting to its current size, we did have one neighborhood group that came in force to dispute a multi-family fire safety standard enacted in conjunction with our licensing requirement. As soon as we recognized that we had a special group with their own issue, we went to plan #2. The mayor chaired the traditional town meeting with the folks that had arrived for that purpose. With an assist from the building and zoning director, I convened with the multi-family folks in an adjoining room. The night was a "success" for everyone.

Neighborhood Dialogues

As just noted, the town meeting attempts to encourage a neighborly character to the gathering. The neighborhood dialogue carries this concept forward one step further. These neighborhood meetings are conducted three times each year and rotate around eight school attendance areas. Individual invitations are directed to each household for the meeting in their neighborhood. The purpose of the neighborhood dialogue is to literally bring village government to the neighborhood and to inform residents about the array of services and facilities available in the village. It is also an opportunity to answer questions that residents may have about village services and once again engage citizens on how to improve the quality of the village and its services.

The mayor emcees the meeting which is also attended by trustees and key staff members to field questions. The dialogue begins with a PowerPoint presentation on village services. The park district provides a similar video. Other taxing bodies such as the school district, library, and fire district are also invited to participate. Attendees at the meeting are documented and minutes of the meeting are prepared and sent to each attendee. Answers to all questions are included in the minutes. Questions that require further information or follow-up are also updated and included in the minutes. Attendees at the dialogues will go into the database for invitations to the town meeting and other citizen participation events, such as public meetings for development of the comprehensive plan or the neighborhood strategy area plan.

Principles Tying Together Citizen Engagement

These three activities--CNS, town meeting, and dialogues--are basics in the annual strategic management process designed to encourage citizen engagement. What are some of the reasons that these activities are successful? First, the topic is important to people, and, for their effort, village officials and staff will hear them. To paraphrase a pop principle, "if you hear them, they will come." Second, this process is straightforward and inclusive. You don't need special status. In fact, you are encouraged to attend because of one key fact; you are a member of this community. Third, issues that are brought to any of these forums are addressed. Input is evaluated and people are told about the results of the process.

Residents are told about steps to implement their input and periodically the long term impact of citizen input is assessed. Every third or fourth year, the town meeting focuses on the long term impact of participation in the meeting, and its impact on community decisions and direction. This is really the true test if people are being heard. What did this collective group of residents conclude at prior meetings and how has village government responded? Fourth, citizens are engaged because the process is timely. The traditional strategic planning process looks at a three, five, or ten year time horizon. Residents who are interested in the long term welfare of their community are willing to engage more frequently and will pay attention to regular reports on the progress of their community.

Before we turn to the two components of what and how we accomplished citizen engagement through our employees, I want to underscore the synergy between citizens and public servants—elected officials and employees alike. I want to highlight this synergy by sharing an experience that I had during a key juncture in my career. This experience heralds a special part of the citizen—public servant relationship that is essential to a positive career and rejuvenating encounters with citizens along the way.

Citizens—the Manager's Sparkplug

In Park Forest in early 1987, we were in the first stages of implementing the redevelopment plan for the Park Forest Plaza. This was a project that the community considered crucial to its ongoing health and sustenance. The Plaza, one of the first American malls, was anchored by Sears and Marshall Fields. It had shown signs of aging and was not as well-positioned as other newer malls on higher traffic arterials or near Interstate interchanges. The Plaza had gone through three foreclosures or bankruptcies over the prior decade.

In 1986, the village reached a redevelopment agreement with a Baltimore developer to undertake a $20 million redevelopment of the Plaza. The village had pledged substantial support through tax increment financing (TIF), including a specially crafted sales tax TIF. The physical redevelopment began fall 1986. I sent off the first payment to the developer in early January 1987 after consulting with the appropriate staff to confirm that all the development targets had been met. I was in good spirits as I departed for Washington D.C. to talk with our Congressional representatives from Illinois.

The Washington visit was part of an ongoing campaign by Park Forest and other south suburban and diverse Chicago-area communities to sensitize HUD to the impact of foreclosed homes. The day began with a wake-up well before dawn and an early flight to D.C. We had several meetings with members of the House and Senate. We gained their pledge to appeal to HUD to better maintain foreclosed properties, cooperate with sales to communities interested in purchases of foreclosures, and to encourage the distribution of Section 8 certificates in accordance with the ideals of the program. The day was encouraging, but this had already been a multi-year effort to gain this consideration.

The trip home started early in the evening and was routed through Newark airport. A problem with connecting flights caused the trip home to be delayed a couple hours. I arrived home shortly before midnight. As I opened the door, my wife handed me an envelope from the village. Her expression didn't convey a look of enthusiasm, and certainly dampened my excitement of returning home. I opened the envelope and found a memo from the deputy manager to the board. The memo explained that earlier in the day the village had received notice from Marshall Fields indicating its intent to leave its store in Park Forest Plaza. This news, on top of the events of the day, now wore very heavily on my usual positive approach to life. The news was devastating, and I felt its full impact.

The next morning I went in to the village hall at the usual time. I do not ever recall being as pessimistic, and probably depressed, as that morning. The Plaza redevelopment was critical. It suddenly looked like it was not going to happen. A pall hung over the atmosphere in the building. I certainly wasn't moving in any positive direction, much less considering what options were available to the village, when I got an unanticipated visitor.

The Tea Goes Into the Harbor

The visitor was Matt, a gentleman who I had met in the last year. Matt lived about a block from me on Westwood Drive. He always spoke positively about the community. Matt moved to Park Forest so that he could be near his grandkids that lived in Park Forest. Matt came in and he was quite animated. "How could Marshall Fields do this?" he asked. This type of behavior was not appropriate for the number one retailer in the Chicago area, Matt added. Did the company understand the impact that a pullout would have on Park Forest? This just was not fair. I can still picture him as he wound up his speech. I was starting to become more involved in acknowledging his points. When he came to the end of his soliloquy, Matt posed the call to arms. Matt finished with a well known question. "John, isn't it time to throw the tea in the harbor?" He concluded. I wasn't in Boston, but I felt like it for a moment. Matt had changed my emotional state.

My outlook was quickly focused and redirected to the options at hand. I consulted with our communications staff and we agreed to convene a meeting with residents to see what interest existed to protest the actions of Marshall Fields. I spoke with the developer to gain his insight and determine what steps might be taken to resolve this situation. I followed up with the mayor and village attorney to gain their guidance. Another staff group began to explore county and state level political and funding support to remedy some of the barriers identified during these early conversations.

The next month was the most intense in my professional career. Those interested residents numbered about 200. They organized daily protests and picketing at the downtown flagship store for Marshall Fields. We did identify some additional financial support for the project to provide added "perks" for Fields. The third prong of our strategy was to prepare to file a class action against the company for alleged discriminatory practices. We prosecuted these strategies diligently. The community was overjoyed when, in early February, Philip Miller, Marshall Fields Chief Executive, announced that Fields had agreed to extend its lease ten years. Park Forest had avoided a bullet and we could complete the redevelopment project that the community saw as crucial.

My motivation and initiative was spurred by Matt showing up in my office—when I most needed the emotional boost. I had been affirmed and transformed by this citizen. The simple point is that we need to recognize our need for this citizen approval, this granting of license, and this bolstering of the professional manager's psyche. The professional should not be the object of derision nor the scapegoat for public attack and sacrifice. This story highlights how professional and citizen are collaborators in support of the community mission and goals. The Field's story was a crisis. How can we sustain the commitment and engagement of citizens beyond crises situations?

Sustained Citizen Engagement

The values, structures, and processes the elected officials have supported for citizen engagement in Woodridge provide a great opportunity to connect to the 35,000 plus residents and accomplish the impossible mission. The element of the relationship with our stakeholders that I will talk about at length is the need to engage with our citizens through their daily contacts with employees. The citizen engagement process and structure must rely upon mutual support and seeing all the parties as partners in the building of community. Citizen engagement means that residents are connected to their community, citizens and government are solving problems together. Citizens are not spectators or complainants – they are contributors to quality programs and improved service.

Citizens are involved because they are part of the community. Those who want to be actively involved in village government need an objective or purpose. Those residents in Park Forest who worked to save Marshall Fields had an objective or purpose. If every community would be able to have such a clear objective, I imagine that the job of governance, and the success of a community, would be much easier. Woodridge has been able to provide this purpose through focusing on the mission and goals of its strategic management process. The objective or purpose of citizen engagement is the same as all the other players in the organization. Having a purpose—and particularly having a <u>unity</u> in that purpose—magnifies the opportunity for great results.

Employee Engagement— Connecting Citizens Geometrically

What are the key building blocks for establishing this climate of citizen engagement and especially linking the key engagers—the employees who provide the point of contact on a constant basis? In order for community building to occur through strategic management and other established processes and structures, the organization's culture has to be primed to participate. A few years back we talked with the department managers and supervisors in Woodridge about what they thought helped us value resident input, motivate customer service, and embrace citizen engagement. We saw several themes emerge from that conversation. I will first describe the four elements that contributed to the component of "how" employees are motivated to embrace a citizen engagement/service culture. I will then turn to the component of "what" we did to support that impetus.

Empowering Employees so They Can Serve

The first component is empowering employees. This deals with how employees are motivated. Employees at all levels must have decision making responsibility appropriate to their task. Sometimes we hear this as pushing responsibility downward—it really means pushing downward the authority to accomplish the mission. With increased responsibility and the authority to carry it out, employees gain confidence in their ability to handle many situations. Department managers' role here is to provide for that capacity by helping the employee set goals and removing any obstacles and gaining support by bringing in additional stakeholders.

Decision making responsibilities build confidence when they are reinforced through the daily service expectations and role of the employee. Empowered employees are part of the process. They have direct contact with the resident when they have to write a traffic ticket, terminate water service, or inspect a newly installed fence. They also need to participate in critical policy and community networking settings. Employees in Woodridge will attend and be actively involved in the town meeting and the neighborhood dialogue. Employees can facilitate discussion with residents and also assist with the resolution, or follow-up, on specific problems that surface. Residents generally are appreciative of these efforts and respond positively to this setting for problem solving.

Mission and Values as Guide for Superior Service

The second theme apparent in the culture was that expectations are made clear through a mission statement or value statement. I talked earlier about the "elegance" of our mission statement and how it is widely and routinely communicated. This helps to convey to employees how they are expected to provide service—in a superior manner. Department managers believe that over time the attitude of employees has changed to be more positive. How is this reflected? Police supervisors explained that they expect officers to look to nonverbal communication clues when working with residents. If there is even a clue that the resident needs assistance, they are expected to ask. As a regular observer on police ride-alongs, I can attest to the finesse and insight shown by officers in their field contacts.

In public works, employees are not only expected to fulfill work orders but they are encouraged to create a dialogue with residents. Even when the issue is not the responsibility of the department, the employee is expected to provide assistance and make the connection to someone who can assist. In the planning and development department, employees understand that they will often be serving people who have limited knowledge of the complex development and zoning process. These employees see their role with residents as the teachers on planning issues, and, if they become the students in the process, that's even better.

Key to assimilating into the culture is helping the employee understand the big picture. The more a manager communicates how each employee has an important role to accomplish the organization's mission, generally the better communication and better service to the resident. Feedback from our senior building inspector following his facilitation training and participation in his first town meeting was that he truly understood how he did fit into the big picture. He has since been promoted to department manager and leads weekly meetings that address departmental issues. He urges his staff to take on a global perspective by asking the question "How does what your doing fit in to what the village is trying to achieve?" After starting this technique, he noted that an inspector came up to him and provided an update and said, "see, I'm thinking globally."

Global Mission—It's Personal

One of the building and zoning inspectors was involved in a very memorable example of how an employee can fulfill the "global mission" through his everyday activities. The specific incident involved a home that was the subject of a long grass complaint. This inspector handled the matter the first time that it was reported in accordance with the standard procedure. The homeowner was issued a notice which was ignored. After several attempts to get the homeowner to mow the lawn, the inspector ordered the village contractor to mow the property. The property was liened to pay for the cost of mowing.

A similar scenario played out at this home the following year. Although the inspector had expected the problem to reoccur and he took early action to motivate the homeowner, the homeowner still allowed the grass to grow beyond the permitted level, notices were issued, and the grass was mowed by the village contractor. Neighbors were increasingly frustrated by the problem. Despite village responsiveness, the neighbors would have preferred an owner who met his obligation. As this summer progressed, the inspector became more active in understanding why this problem repeated. Working with the police department and neighbors, he learned that the offending resident exhibited some unusual behaviors. The unusual behaviors probably were tied to an emotional condition. This resident was not capable of caring for his own needs.

The inspector was encouraged to find a way to assist. Through property transaction records, he was able to reach a sister of the "disabled" occupant and explain what had been happening. He was able to convince an Ohio sister to come and help. The sister was able to obtain the necessary institutional care for her brother and she also sold the property. The neighbors, village, and most importantly the person who needed help were all served in the best way possible. A management consultant that provides some coaching to our department managers met with the building and zoning employees a couple days later. He described this result to me and simply said, "a miracle." I was familiar with the history, but hadn't attached such a superlative—but after thinking about it—I now describe this example as the "miracle"

Complaints as Service Opportunities

The third component of establishing a culture of service and citizen engagement in the organization is to establish that every complaint or concern is an opportunity to create a dialogue and prove the superior service target is real. Part of this process also depends upon removing the "victim" from the service scenario. We are all familiar with how some encounters between residents and municipal employees are stereotyped. The resident may start with how he or she has suffered some loss and it is "all the fault of the municipal government." The employee, on the other hand, might adopt the perspective that he has encountered a resident who can't be satisfied because of a negative view of government. If we have a "victim," then we have a problem that is much harder to solve.

We need to change how these encounters are perceived and approached. I have a good example on how the public works department has "repositioned" one of its routine citizen contacts. During the winter time, one of the unintended consequences of plowing snow is that a snowplow may hit a mailbox, requiring its replacement. This will usually occur when snow accumulates and large amounts of snow are pushed behind the curb line, right where the curbside mailbox is located on its post. This event is one that normally strains feelings between the resident and the plow driver. It usually occurs in the midst of long shifts by the public works employee and some extra work and inconvenience experienced by the resident.

The department has taken a different approach to this situation. The employees with support from the supervisory staff decided that every time a mailbox was hit to turn it into a good thing. The employee is encouraged to talk to the resident and tell them that a temporary mailbox will go in until the permanent one is installed, soon after winter conditions subside.

The best example of how this changed the service encounter between employee and resident came during my last week of employment. I received a long e-mail from a resident thanking the public works department for the thoughtful, and somewhat unexpected, replacement of her mail box. The satisfied resident lived on the route that I had taken to work everyday for twenty years. She explained that she works very hard to maintain her home in top condition so that she was concerned when the special mailbox that she had installed recently was destroyed. This lady explained that she had not expected the replacement box.

I visited this home on my way home to see why this lady was so overwhelmingly pleased with her contact with public works. I drove up to the home and immediately understood why she was so positive. The replacement box, while not expensive and within the allowance for replacement, was a special wrought iron design. The empowered employee had used this encounter as an opportunity to engage a resident and prove that the village is sensitive to resident concerns and does provide superior services.

Model Effective Citizen Servants

Another component of the citizen engagement, citizen service culture is to lead by example and mirror the successful practitioner. One of the department managers explained in our informal survey that they felt that not only were the mayor and the administrator good leaders and examples of valuing resident input, but so were fellow department managers. This manager explained how he was frustrated by how he sometimes handled citizen complaints. When he witnessed how other managers handled complaints at a neighborhood dialogue, he saw that managers were empathetic, but separated the emotions from the issue and provided an effective response to dealing with the issue. For this manager, who had many years of experience, it was a big step forward in understanding how to be effective and raise his comfort level in future similar encounters.

We have all heard reference to "walking the talk"—the need not only to talk, but to follow through with supportive action. Modeling effective citizen engagement and service leads us right into the responsibility of the manager to provide resources and other support to capture, and maintain, the benefits of motivated employees. We have three elements that support this component of how we facilitate employees engaging citizens.

Share Tools for Performance through Training

Training is an important element of building the engagement culture. Training is highly valued by the mayor and board. Trustees have made commentary about how they like reading about the training attended by employees because they are continuously building upon their skills. Through the administrator's memorandum, the Board can see the training and many of the incidents that show its value. How does the employee learn about what is expected and valued and in what ways an employee can perform the task, especially citizen engagement? One tool that Woodridge uses to assimilate the value of residential dialogue is through facilitation training. A manager or supervisor will normally, in his or her first six months, be sent to this training that focuses on skills for building consensus, focused conversation, and action planning. These tools are utilized at town meeting for gathering input from residents.

Hire a Service Believer

Department managers consider the hiring decision as a major theme in building a culture that values resident input. The process itself--the job description, interview questions, and problem solving scenarios--should focus on customer service and addressing resident need. When interviewing prospective employees, I found success was dependent on having multiple inputs, more than one person making the assessment. The multiple perspectives add rigor and redundancy to the process. Asking questions such as does the applicant seem willing to confront issues and does the employee have a human perspective in the decision making process? The inspector who performed the "miracle" had a human perspective. These are important considerations in determining if the applicant would be a good fit for Woodridge.

Learn from Those with Citizen Connections

Feedback is another crucial component building a culture open to citizen engagement and customer service. First of all, the organization must strive to inform all the internal participants. This must be done routinely and regularly. There need to be a variety of tools used, and they need to be coordinated, as least containing messages that are not inconsistent. One tool that is used to inform department managers and employees as well as the mayor and board is the weekly administrator's memorandum. The administrator's memorandum is a weekly snapshot of key information related to managing and governing the community. Whenever possible, the AM includes information on specific "good deeds" of employees in the field.

A crucial component of feedback is directly measuring citizen perception of the performance. Every administrator or manager is encouraged to provide regular verbal feedback when good performance is observed and this expectation is likewise passed along to departments and in turn the supervisors. However, the organization gains when this "verbal" feedback is routinely structured and shared more broadly. The police and public works departments distribute a citizen evaluation survey randomly to residents who have been recently serviced. The results of these surveys are compiled regularly into a semi-annual report and shared with the mayor and board and the rest of the organization through the administrator's memorandum.

The public works department takes it a step further and mails a copy of the report to all of its employees – thanking them for their efforts. Employees are asked to share the results with their family in appreciation for the sacrifices provided during times with extended work hours, such as a snow storm or holiday call-out for a water main repair.

Employees Do the Work—Value Them

Reinforcing positive performance through recognizing and rewarding is important and key to sustaining a culture that values citizen engagement and service. It is done in many ways, through the weekly AM, during the management team meeting which includes a good news agenda item, and within each department. Every department has a method of recognizing the efforts of its employees. Managers set aside time in their meetings to recognize the efforts of employees and thank them for a job well done. The larger departments, police and public works, have a formal recognition program that identifies top performers and special incidents that demonstrate extraordinary efforts to carry out the department mission, village mission, and provide outstanding citizen service. The village also has a formal recognition program where employees vote for employee of the quarter and employee of the year.

Double Dutch--Empowered Citizens and Employees Jump to Build Community

I would like to highlight one of the examples of citizen engagement that shows the power that this process or attitude conveys to all persons involved in the equation. We will be able to see how employee empowerment supports good customer service which leads to effective citizen engagement and, in this case, clearly reinforces the benefits to community building on an ongoing basis.

Two residents in Woodridge felt that there was a strong need for programs for young teens in the village. These residents also saw a need for programs that involved the parents of these teens. They wanted to provide some exposure to leaders in the community to this need and this opportunity. The two women had no idea how to mobilize the community to provide these much needed activities.

One of these residents remembered her experience with a Woodridge police officer about six years before. She had been impressed by how effectively and sensitively the officer had handled very difficult issues with some youth. The officer, who had been given special responsibility for the neighborhood of particular interest to these residents, had continued to build a rapport in this area. This resident approached the officer and soon police department representatives were meeting with the two women. The chief and the officer told the group that they would support this initiative, but it would be their responsibility to develop the activities and programs. These residents enrolled others for their group and formed the Agents for Change.

Agents for Change designed several programs such as a neighborhood barbeque and teen activity survey, a double dutch tournament, and a three-on-three basketball tournament. When one of the residents was asked about what most surprised her about the process of developing these programs, she said that she was surprised by two things. First, she did not expect that the department and the mayor trusted her to create solutions to fill the need, and each party supported the programs by raising funding to carry them out. Second, she was surprised by the fact that "two old ladies can come to the village for help in filling a need and the result is a series of very successful programs for the youth in the community."

One of those ladies is now a village trustee and has increased her successful involvement and commitment to the community. She is also an advocate for citizen engagement which empowers citizens and employees and continues to contribute to build community.

Expand the Rich Community Network

Effective community leaders, good managers included, readily understand that they can't do everything and some things they can't do as well as others. However, you had better find the person or group who <u>can</u> do those things. I have talked about enlisting citizens through engagement in building community. I want to broaden that understanding of "citizens" and turn to the need to work with all stakeholder groups. You need to see how far you can extend the cadre, the network, of community builders.

More Bricks to Build Community

In both Woodridge and Park Forest, leaders recognized the benefit of a strong and active Chamber of Commerce. Active participation in local chambers usually revolves around small businesses and professionals. These people are probably not just businesses---but often are also residents who have a bigger financial investment in the community than the average resident. The Chamber needs to be part of the network, because they are your most productive connection to the business community. The Chamber leadership wants to know about issues in the community. They can help educate their membership. The Village needs to know what the Chamber sees as issues for the business community.

Building the community through this Chamber-Village government connection requires some manager time—the players change regularly and business cycles change the issues. You need to devote quality time. If you don't have enough time, you will have staff members who appreciate the opportunity. Make sure that they understand how important it is. If you demonstrate a commitment to the Chamber, they will become "partner leaders" in building community. You will be able to replicate this approach with many other stakeholder groups.

As a young community, Woodridge supported the development of, and connection to, service clubs. Woodridge Rotary formed two months after I arrived in Woodridge. I have been a member ever since. The Woodridge board has supported membership by elected officials and employees in all community organizations. How better to be connected—gaining greater volunteer support and "kinship" with those whom you are serving. I noted in my retirement resignation letter that:

> "Each of the employees with whom I served during these 20 years is a source of pride. They are compassionate, willing to volunteer their time and regularly contribute to help others in the community."

We gained so much through the connection of elected officials and employees in community service organizations. The non-profit Culture Fest Committee is supported by a significant number of employees.

I learned the importance of local realtors in shaping the real estate market and shaping opinion when I was in Park Forest. In both communities, we conducted an annual tour of the village with local realtors. This is a great opportunity to inform key players what is happening in the community— get them involved early in new developments and issues. In Woodridge, we programmed open seats on the bus to include employees who might normally be "stuck in the office" everyday. Both realtors and employees gave the tour high marks. As we will review in communications chapter, you are "doing good things, then tell people." Woodridge also hosted a Corporate Classic golf outing in the late 80s and early 90s. The Classic appealed to non-residential developers—when you own a golf course why not take 100 of your development stakeholders for golf and a pitch about the community over lunch.

In my first years in Woodridge, we undertook a program of improvement through convening various focus groups to provide programmatic input and gain a sense of what residents thought about the current conditions and efforts of the village. Groups were convened to give feedback on streetscape, especially tree planting and care, and community image. These groups of "specialists" were a precursor for the work that we undertook with the Quality Community Task Force and eventually the town meeting.

These community conversations were a great opportunity to engage interested residents in providing feedback on: (1) how we were seen; (2) how we were performing; and (3) how we could do better. In the case of each focus group, we tried to gather together people who had a general interest or were experts in the field in the non-governmental sector. We gained insight into what we might try to become better in each of the functions reviewed. More importantly, we were learning a process of how to engage residents in meaningful dialogue and we were learning, in a closer more intimate way, what our residents thought about the community. In the case of each focus group that was established, we began to broaden the group of people who had ownership for what was happening in the community.

Many Governments—Same Community

Illinois has a "special" reputation amongst the states of the union. Illinois has more units of local government than any state. Both Woodridge and Park Forest are served by at least six school districts. A municipal library, with an independent board, serves both communities. Park Forest has a village recreation and parks department; Woodridge has a park district which is a separate government entity. Park Forest has a fire department; Woodridge has three fire districts. The list is more extensive—but you get the point. These government entities are another group of "citizens" that you need to be at your side in building community.

These other government entities are a real source of "partner leaders." They each have their constituency which to some degree will match the constituency of village government. Given their diversity and numbers, how do you engage them in building community? You need to spend time getting to know their leaders. You need to educate them about the village mission. You need to identify issues for the community around which they can assist. You need to identify issues important to these other governmental entities and how your village strategy supports their needs.

Every form of citizen engagement begins with the village mission. The mission is the platform from which all connections are made. In both Woodridge and Park Forest, I met with a group of government administrators periodically to review progress on the village mission, explain strategies, share information, and identify issues that might enhance cooperation or generate conflict.

The Woodridge get together was known as the quarterly administrators meeting. This group included the park district, largest high school district, the two largest grade school districts, the library, and three Fire districts. This meeting was reasonably successful. What was most successful was the participation by these administrators, their staffs, and the elected officials from these government entities in the strategic management process. We had a significant contribution from these players at the town meeting, neighborhood dialogues, and other special meetings involving citizens. The mayor acknowledges their participation at every public opportunity and shows his sincere appreciation for their efforts.

Imitation is the Highest Compliment

Perhaps the best indication of the connection of the Woodridge government bodies was the use of citizen engagement processes by several of the other government bodies in this group. The largest grade school district and the park district now consistently use forms of strategic planning with significant citizen involvement. The mayor, administrator, and other village officials participate in these events and have an opportunity by which to understand decisions of these other government bodies and a perfect opportunity to give input for their policy decisions.

Citizens expect to live in a community that works. The connections amongst these government bodies are often noted by the residents in Woodridge. The comment that "I've lived in several communities and I have never seen the level of communication and cooperation that exists here in Woodridge," is often voiced in the community needs survey and at neighborhood dialogues. You can imagine the pride of the residents and how this experience reinforces their commitment to working together to build community.

Bridges to Diverse Citizens

Citizen engagement doesn't build community unless it includes everyone. We all know that our communities are becoming more diverse. I have shared salient portions of the history of diversity in Park Forest. Park Forest's has been addressing diversity issues for 50 years—nearly its entire history. Woodridge has African American, Asian, and Latino populations each over 10 percent. If you want to successfully build community and engage citizens, you must find ways to include these diverse populations. You will need to consider special "tactics" to bring diverse groups on board, but bring them on board you must.

The message to citizens in your community is conveyed in many ways. As a diverse community, Woodridge set a goal "to improve ethnic and race relations by creating a healthy and positive atmosphere among all residents." A goal is a start. More needs to be done to demonstrate movement toward that goal. The community resource center (CRC) is Woodridge's most significant programmatic effort to support inclusion and engagement for all citizens. The CRC offers after-school, summer camp, English as a second language, computer skills, and parenting support for the whole community, but in a neighborhood that is more diverse.

The engagement of residents and perceptions of this neighborhood have improved measurably since the CRC was established. The CRC has brought people together to give them a setting to help each other. The CRC spearheaded the Latino Outreach program which helped get out service information to the Latino community. Five intergovernmental organizations worked together to produce this outreach program. CRC kids were a part of the award-winning "Dancing with the CRC Kids" program. The CRC is a great source of talent and residents who we can add to an engaged community.

Another message to the diverse citizenry came through the study circles on diversity. This small group dialogue involved more than 100 residents in weekly conversations about their heritage and backgrounds, how to build trusting relationships, and what solutions might be effective for the community. The study circles were designed, and convened through, the leadership of the churches in the community. We worked to engage a diverse community through engaging the local churches—to build community for all. We also learned that church bulletins can be an effective way to connect with residents.

High profile, social events are another way to engage a diverse population. The Woodridge Culture Fest is designed to be a celebration of ethnic diversity in the community. The town centre is adorned with 40 flags of countries from all around the world. The two day festival featuring foods and entertainment from Woodridge's different cultures is a symbol for the entire community that everyone in the community is valued in the creation of a community vision.

Reaching Beyond

Park Forest has been more noteworthy than Woodridge in its pursuit of racial equity on the regional and national stage. Such high profile efforts have an impact on sending a message to a widespread diverse audience. Thanks to my experience in Park Forest, and with help from former staff members, I was able to share some of that background and experience with colleagues in DuPage after I relocated to Woodridge. The DuPage Mayors and Managers Conference (DMMC) used this information to establish a strategic plan for sustainable, diverse communities.

My experience in Park Forest inscribed upon me the value of multi-municipal cooperation. The pursuit of racial justice was the most exceptional example. Having been a totally planned community, Park Forest responded with great diligence to regional issues. Even before becoming a manager, I had support from my mentor to help form the Intergovernmental Risk Management Agency (IRMA), labor relations education (IPELRA), and pooled bond financing.

When I came to Woodridge, I had the good fortune of partnering with a mayor who already had proven his commitment to multi-municipal initiatives. The mayor, with a significant assist from the village attorney, led the municipal coalition that formed the DuPage Water Commission (DWC). He was a frequent participant on County task forces and study groups that reviewed drugs, gangs, and the efficiency and effectiveness of local government services. The mayor also chaired the DMMC and the Illinois Municipal League (IML). Once again, I had the good fortune of being partnered with a mayor who wanted the best for Woodridge—and understood that it might require perseverance and hard work to engage stakeholders beyond Woodridge's borders.

My partnership with the mayor required that I support him in his multi-municipal initiatives and, in some cases, he support mine. We shared the same goal whoever was in the lead. Because of the mayor's history with the DWC, Woodridge became embroiled in a major battle with DuPage County when the DuPage County Board Chair decided to try to takeover the water agency. If the County Board Chair could access money accumulated by DWC, he could balance his budget. The mayor and I helped to bring together the charter member municipalities to resist this "hijacking." A manager from another DuPage community used to comment that "John didn't realize that the other managers in DuPage were not on the Woodridge staff." I took this as a compliment, especially given my respect for the work of that manager. Often times what is needed is for the multi-municipal group to come together like they were performing as a high-performing staff team.

Managers need to understand that they must commit time to multi-municipal activities. This arena is too important to the success of building each community. Whatever the priorities on the "home front" that may require your attention, you need to initiate, nurture, and sustain the capacity to act with cities beyond your borders. That does not mean getting involved only when the issue directly impacts your community. It means committing to your regional COG, your state municipal league, and other special service agencies. It means providing support to your partner municipalities who are taking the lead on any particular issue through these intergovernmental agencies.

CHAPTER 6

STRATEGIES FOR BUILDING COMMUNITY

Village Mission—The Positive Self-Fulfilling Prophecy

Some argue that government is different than the private sector. We in local government, however, are shadowed by some of basic capitalist notions—"nothing succeeds like success;" "it's all about the bottom line;" and "show me the results." These popular maxims are all reflective of the pressures that communities and their managers face. An effective manager must bring positive results to his or her community. What did I learn about getting the bottom line results for my community during my career? How did I work to bring together all the pieces to build community?

I will outline in this chapter the building blocks for community building that relate to getting bottom line results. We will talk about developing a "positive self-fulfilling prophecy," a mission, which can become the focus for all in the community, and guide their common efforts. As I outline these building blocks to produce the bottom line results of community building, I will be recounting how this transition occurred in Woodridge. As we noted in the opening chapter, we don't make progress in community building in leaps and bounds. We build community one step at a time--often in "baby steps." This is an incremental process—built on the foundation already "poured." I will conclude by providing an over-arching summary of the strategic management process and additional examples as to how it changed the Woodridge community.

Another Lesson Learned From Park Forest

Since my service in Park Forest was many years ago, I have already explained what I took with me from that experience. I also reach back to those formative years when I learned the principle to manage for a "positive self-fulfilling prophecy."

In Park Forest, I had the pleasure and opportunity to work with two other assistants to the village manager who had extraordinary talent and ability, one headed the youth service function and the other was responsible for human and community relations. The assistant for community relations, who often found himself at the point of conflict and controversy, repeatedly tried to guide and lead by emphasizing the positive result that people working together could accomplish. He constantly talked about the "positive, self-fulfilling prophecy." I watched and learned in Park Forest from his regular application of this principle with many small groups and always in difficult situations.

Individuals, teams, and organizations must have a "positive, self-fulfilling prophecy" in order to guide their actions. Our focus upon community building, and as the overriding "positive self-fulfilling prophecy," dictates that we establish a mission to guide us. We discussed the importance of the mission in engaging elected officials, citizens and employees around the cause of community building. Sometimes it is easier to get people to focus or refocus upon the mission—"the bigger picture" by simply reminding them that we need to work toward a "positive, self-fulfilling prophecy" and show how their efforts will make an important contribution.

There are several key benefits to having a simple mission or slogan to guide each group of stakeholders and the full community. First, you can see where it is that you want to end up, even if the full mission is not yet established or your audience is not yet conversant with the mission. Second, you better understand how to align all your activities around this mission; it becomes an organizing principle for all contributors. All activities are assessed by measuring the impact upon the mission. Third, when criticism or "noise" occurs around an issue, all the stakeholders have some basis by which to judge the value of what is generating the concern.

Taking Care of Business Before Formulating the Woodridge Mission

When I relocated to Woodridge, one of the first issues on my list was to find a project or task that was visible to the mayor and board and get it accomplished. A manager will often have to begin working toward results while he is still sorting out how everything fits together in his new community. I wanted to produce results that the community considered important—pursue a "positive self-fulfilling prophecy" even if the "bigger picture" mission was not yet clearly articulated.

I was immediately thrust into negotiating an annexation agreement for a 500 acre development. The developer was also the owner of a water utility company that served Woodridge and portions of neighboring community Darien. Acquiring the water system was a part of the village's strategy for providing services and increased the likelihood of accomplishing additional annexations. Committing substantial time to this annexation, we were able to accomplish this annexation and utility purchase within six months of my arrival in Woodridge. My early activities helped "fulfill the prophecy."

Strategies to Fulfill the Prophecy

My work on this annexation provided me with a number of clues as to what was important to the mayor and board and what broader objectives existed for the community. The community had the ability to grow, probably to twice the size, geographically and population, beyond what existed in 1989. The village board saw this growth as part of the "diversification" of the community.

The annexed area provided the opportunity for the community to add significant numbers of new, higher cost single family homes to Woodridge. The annexed area permitted the development of key traffic arteries that would help to move traffic along the route of the new toll highway extension- -and feed the three interchanges within Woodridge. The annexed area provided over 100 acres of land for non-residential development. This land could someday be developed for office and retail businesses. This land would provide substantial tax benefits without generating school users--the largest expense supported by municipal property taxes.

This annexation would also provide contiguity to other parcels within the village's planning area that could also be annexed to the village. This annexation provided the opportunity to work with the developer to buy the water utility and plan for service extension to the remainder of the village's planning area and ultimate borders. Thus, it was possible to conclude that Woodridge wanted to grow and wanted to effectively serve the new territory. Probably the number one lesson, however, was that the village sought to find ways to accomplish a more balanced tax base. Growth was good, but it needed to yield a tax base that would be more sustainable for future residents. Park Forest thirty years before had decided not to grow and, as I noted in Chapter 2, suffered the consequences of having limited opportunity to expand its tax base. Woodridge was working to find resources to sustain its economic base to fund its future needs—pursuing the strategy of investing in projects that would improve the community capacity to flourish.

Credibility to Move Forward

My early success was a platform from which to undertake further management initiatives and build credibility with my new employer. It was valuable to confirm the faith that the mayor and board placed in me at time of hiring. The manager should use this "credibility capital" to build greater capacity in order to pursue long term results that will build the community.

Reality or the Twilight Zone

In chapter 2, I talked about the importance of understanding the community's character or personality, knowing what a community stands for and what it wants to become. In the first six months in Woodridge, I learned a lot about what "made the community tick." Yet, I felt that it was important to learn more and try to stake out how the mayor, trustees, and key staff saw the "self-fulfilling prophecy" for Woodridge.

One of the important lessons of management that has become clearer to me over time is that whatever principles or objectives the manager might assume, hold, or believe, and are a product of the direction that he believes has been given, those principles need to be checked, double-checked, reinforced, reiterated, reviewed, and renewed--both up and down the line. Clarifying and communicating what the organization hopes to achieve may be the most important task for the administrator to accomplish. If all the players are going to "get on the same page," you need a simple standard from which to judge issues that arise. You need to clarify your "positive self-fulfilling prophecy" more rigorously as a mission statement so that you can more clearly communicate what the community will look like as you seek to build community--the "ideals and sacred things" of the city.

So let us briefly review the first steps that Woodridge took under my management watch to define the mission and what it hoped to accomplish as a community.

In order to spell out more clearly what the elected officials desired for the community, and begin to paint the picture of what all the stakeholders in the community will become, I considered it necessary to begin a team building and strategic planning process. Strategic planning is not new, nor is it the cure-all for all that ails an organization. It is also not a sure bet to future success. Traditional strategic planning has many shortcomings or tendencies that don't have a track record for sustainable results. The complaints and documented failures of strategic planning in many jurisdictions include (1) plans that are too far into the future to maintain interest; (2) lack of citizen input and involvement after the initial input process; (3) unrealistic, "pie in the sky" blueprints that end up on the shelf; and (4) plans that don't generate budgetary commitments. Despite these pitfalls, we needed to confirm the group's current understanding of its mission and priorities so that we were all aligned and moving in the same direction. Thus, we embarked on strategic planning.

Strategic Management---Strategic Planning on Steroids

Woodridge's version of strategic planning, or as it became known after its first five years, strategic management, proved to be a unifying and clarifying process that was embraced by the mayor and board, management team, employees, and residents as time progressed. What caused strategic management to be this structure that brought together such a broad range of decision-makers and stakeholders? Let's explore the history that produced the strategic management process and supported a long term commitment to successful results that built community.

I saw two important reasons for trying to generate a broader context for achieving results important to Woodridge. First, I found a rigorous planning process in place when I arrived in Woodridge that emphasized goals and objectives for managers throughout the organization. While this structure and practice existed, the management staff complained that it was a "painful" process. The process and structure, best described as management by objectives, started in the early 80s with best intentions, was supported by all the elected officials and appointed managers. Somehow this annual review process, however, became more of an "inquisition." Department managers felt that the focus shifted to explaining the reasons for any changes that were requested for projects or dollars that had not previously been assigned in earlier plans which covered a five year horizon. Lost was an emphasis on the bigger picture.

When I arrived on the scene, Woodridge did not appear to be suffering from a lack of planning or setting out a number of tasks that the organization wanted to accomplish. Quite the contrary, there was an extensive list of "to dos." Many of these tasks had been "on the list" for several years, but had not moved forward. One of the building blocks that was missing was the "positive self-fulfilling prophecy." I think that my simple principle connotes both where we want to go and how we can judge the contributions that everyone makes to the "prophecy."

Building a Lego Man—Necessary Training for Building Community

During that first year in Woodridge, we conducted a simple, facilitated team-building meeting—the precursor to strategic planning--with a respected organizational development consultant that performed successfully in Park Forest and many rural communities in Illinois. We gathered together the mayor, clerk, trustees, and department managers to get to know each other, increase the sense of team, and identify our expectations for how we would work together. We devoted about half the time to doing team exercises.

One of my fondest recollections of the team building was the exercise that required a team to assemble Lego blocks into the figure of a man. There were certain obstacles and limitations, but good planning and communication were needed to be successful in achieving the final product. The mayor, public works director, and I were team members. We were a competitive group and were overjoyed; ecstatic may be more accurate, by not only beating the other teams, but doing it in a time that was better than all groups with whom the facilitator had ever worked.

Making Progress and Having Fun

After all the "fun," we got down to serious business and identified as a group a simple statement as to what the village hoped to accomplish and a list of goals that would help to characterize the broad functional areas that would demonstrate our progress. We left the meeting with a mission (our self-fulfilling prophecy) and a set of goals that helped describe the vision or picture of what we wanted the village to become. This meeting set a wonderful tone for the future, and began building a relationship amongst the broader management team (mayor and board and department managers) that would serve the village for the next two decades and beyond.

That meeting produced a mission statement which has remained in the same form to this day. The mission statement reads:

To Achieve a High Quality of Life By Providing Superior Services in a Fiscally Responsible Manner

Since the mission statement was adopted, it has routinely guided the Village's activities and budgetary decisions each year. At this early stage of my tenure, we also established a list of goals. As our facilitator characterized them, these goals were the descriptors of what we wanted the community to become and often were helpful statements to guide future strategy and planning. The initial set of goals is set forth below:

- Reduce Residential Tax Burden
- Create a Safe Community

- Develop Programs to Increase Citizen Involvement
- Stimulate Business Community
- Achieve Balanced Growth Through Comprehensive Planning
- Provide Adequate Infrastructure
- Priority on Recreation & Open Space in Development Activities
- Attract & Retain Competent Public Employees
- Foster Intergovernmental Cooperation
- Provide Orderly/Safe Traffic Movement
- Establish a Geographic Center
- Maintain Suburban Image
- Promote Affordable Housing
- Enhance Residential Neighborhoods

The village mission and goals set forth above have been in place for nearly twenty years. The first two goals, reducing the tax burden and creating a safe community have been predominant priorities since this process was established. The village's success with both these goals is primarily attributable to successfully aligning personal accountability for their accomplishment. Bear with me as I tell more of the story about how we set the groundwork for establishing this alignment of individuals and organizational operating units.

I was extremely pleased by the first team building/strategy meeting involving mayor and board and staff in Woodridge. We still needed to do some strategic planning, however. During the budget finalization process in my first month in Woodridge, I asked one of the department managers about a list of sixteen projects that was included on the capital list for the capital projects fund.

I was curious about where the money was coming from to pay for these projects. He explained that there was no money for any of the projects. I asked the department manager if there had been any plans formulated to accomplish these projects. He indicated that the staff could do so when the Board decided which projects should be done. I came away from the conversation understanding that there was no proactive plan to "find money" to do these projects.

Finding Ways to Build Community

Although I had high regard for the staff, I saw a real need to work to define their role more broadly than simply waiting for direction from the board. I was pretty sure that the mayor and board wanted guidance on what they should accomplish but, more importantly, wanted ideas on how to get there. There was an opportunity to explore how some of the village priorities might fit into the operating plan and a more detailed strategic planning effort would be in order.

Due to the pressures on staff time created by multiple major annexations and the utility acquisition, the mayor and board accepted my suggestion to bring onboard a consultant to assist the strategic planning process. In late 1989 or 1990, we retained a nationally recognized strategic planning consultant. The consultant's job was to help us formulate a strategy that responded to the village's mission statement and look for ways to accomplish the long list of goals that had recently been articulated. The limited initiative or aggressiveness of staff to provide strategies or options for the board contributed to what the staff had described as a "painful" financial planning process in the years before my arrival in Woodridge.

We worked with the consultant over two cycles--1990 and 1991. My brother had put me in touch with this consultant who authored a chapter in the *Handbook of Public Administration*. I think that there were some pluses and minuses during that period. As I look back, the areas of strength were those that subsequently helped us prepare for problem-solving for the long term. We had laid out the basic mission of the organization and defined a number of goals to pursue in order to fulfill our mission. The staff learned how to be the "out front" functional leaders for the broad village planning and management process. They began to realize that they had the responsibility to provide options to the board—and they began to build the capacity and confidence to follow through. There were two questions that are basic parts of strategic planning that were the biggest elements of our work during my first two years. We spent the bulk of our time in the strategic planning process on two areas--(1) trends and conditions and (2) operating accountability.

Good Data Make Good Decisions

That first period of strategic planning became a terrific opportunity to step back just a little, during a very busy period for all, and view Woodridge at arm's length and take an overview of the world surrounding Woodridge. This is probably one of the first episodes for me in Woodridge of broadly gathering data, and making sure that we had good data to make good decisions, before having to make judgments about strategic actions and budgetary decisions attached to those actions.

We concluded this period of strategic planning with a mission, goals, knowing better what we do, and depicting the environment and challenges that faced the community. The environment in which the community was growing and developing was reasonably well understood by the combined leadership group—the mayor, trustees, department managers, and other key professionals. The short term achievement targets were also on track—particularly focused on (1) annexations to balance the tax base and (2) improving the financial capacity of the village. For the long-term, we strengthened the ability of the full group to develop policy and we saw a definite growth in the capacity of the department management team.

Overview of Strategic Management

I promised to provide an overview of the strategic management process—a process that pulls together planning and operations--and how this community building process has influenced the direction of the community. Each of the elements are conducted or reviewed annually. Here are the basic elements:

Mission. The Village mission has not changed since it was established in 1990. It still is: To achieve a *high* quality of life by providing superior services in a fiscally responsible manner (emphasis added). The mission contains three simple, yet powerful standards. These benchmarks help guide all Woodridge's work, and give the community a common basis for discussion and deliberation—the essence of community and citizenship articulated two millennia ago by Aristotle.

Citizen Engagement. The process is designed to gain meaningful citizen input. The mayor and board take it very seriously. Educating residents, so that they can intelligently deliberate, is part of the process. They listen to, respond to, and try to act upon the priorities communicated by the community in these engagement processes. The first citizen involvement measure in the annual cycle is the Community Needs Survey (CNS

The second citizen involvement measure is the neighborhood dialogue. This local meeting provides considerable background for new and old residents alike. Elected officials entertain any and all questions, including anonymously, from residents. All the answers are shared at the meeting and through minutes that are later mailed to all attendees.

The third, and most prominent, measure for citizen involvement is the annual town meeting. This meeting is held around October 1. It is usually attended by about 200, and includes time for socializing, education, facilitated small group conversations, and deliberations, and finally providing the mayor and board with feedback on issues the small groups identify as important to the community. As part of the outreach to draw in new participants, we encourage the board members to invite folks to the town meeting that may not have previously participated. Village staff will follow-up with written invitations to individuals identified.

Core Service Review. Each village department has established a list of "core services" that are part of its day-to-day operating responsibilities, evaluative measures are included. The strategic management process is intended to be a process for continuous improvement and improvement at the margin, i.e. what incremental improvement will bring the greatest value to the village. There is an attempt to answer the question, "What can we all do to best move us toward our mission?" The core service review helps everyone understand what basic services exist and how they impact the budget process. The review also includes those significant initiatives that are implemented on a multi-department or "cross-cutting" basis. Woodridge staff review the core services with the mayor and board after the first quarter of the fiscal year, immediately before the compilation of the CNS results and about one month before the town meeting. This step in the process helps everyone to have a basic understanding of services and prepare for the decision making process ahead.

Goal Setting. The information gathering, citizen input, evaluation of critical policies, and strategies is all brought together in this annual meeting of the mayor and board. In addition to the elected officials, meeting attendees include the administrator, department managers, assistant department managers, and other key supervisors and professionals. Beginning with this goal setting session in early November, these thirty people will be heavily involved in the process through the finalization of the budget, the following April.

The goal setting session is designed to integrate all the input from citizens and staff to obtain feedback from the mayor and board for general parameters to construct the upcoming budget. The agenda starts with the mayor and board identifying accomplishments and disappointments during the prior year. The board reflects on the town meeting and other citizen input, reviewing the tax rate policy and five year financial projections, and identifying important strategies and policy initiatives, and setting priorities amongst the village goals. This meeting, more than any during the process, provides the board a platform to confirm direction or encourage changes that will be reflected in the budget plan.

Budget. Budget development is a constant process. Informal meetings with all departments are conducted early in the fiscal year (begins May 1) to hear challenges that may be facing each department and what preliminary homework might be done.

Budget finalization begins after the goal setting session. The finance director and village administrator host a "budget insight" meeting with most of the managers and supervisors in all village departments. This meeting: (1) communicates how the organization has performed financially; (2) updates five year projections based upon the audit; (3) projects what financial climate is expected in the year ahead; (4) identifies operating challenges; (5) shares goal priorities set by the board at the goal setting meeting; (6) explains budget submission parameters; and (7) provides an outlook for employee compensation. Depending upon the issue, this meeting will set direction or seek guidance from this key group of operation leaders.

Triple I. The meeting that pulls together the mission and goals on the budgetary side is the ingenuity and idea interchange—the "Triple I" (formerly the "Feeding Frenzy"). This meeting is a group meeting that reviews the strategic objectives and financial objectives. The group works to adjust the budget for the upcoming fiscal year and the next five years in order to live within these objectives. The title of this meeting has changed over the years to reflect a greater emphasis on collaboration and ideas generated by all the participants rather than simply a budget "cutting" meeting. I know of no other community that successfully conducts such an interactive and participatory process as Woodridge. This approach had its early roots in Park Forest.

Budget Workshop. Elected officials and staff members convene in a full day budget workshop the month before budget adoption. This workshop comprehensively reviews strategies, revenues, special projects, cross-cutting goals (those involving special multi-department efforts), and the impact of all these initiatives measured against the five year financial targets.

I suspect that managers will judge the 2009-10 budget as the most challenging and "taxing," no pun intended, in their experience. The need to consider and make changes in the municipal budget was never so dramatic. The strategic management process, with the underpinning of the village mission and goals, allowed Woodridge to successfully navigate the turbulent financial times. At my final budget workshop, I used the following words to describe the effort---thoughtfulness, ingenuity, sacrifice, unselfishness, teamwork, and building community.

Annual Evaluation of Process. The experience of the board and staff going through the 12 month cycle is evaluated and discussed within sixty days following budget approval. This is an opportunity for all to share what worked successfully and what could be improved. What special focus should the next year take? What do we want to ask our residents as we move forward? There is an attempt to look forward and keep the process fresh, interesting, and evocative of future citizen engagement.

Strategic Management--Contributions to Community Building

I will now try to recap how the strategic management process has helped Woodridge maintain positive movement toward its mission. The mission remains the same. The goals of the community have largely remained the same since the process started. I will provide my summary of "success" based upon the simple benchmarks of the mission statement.

Fiscally responsible. The community has made dramatic progress financially. The village's property tax rate has declined for 23 years. An average homeowner pays the same amount of property tax each year, about $220, that it paid 15 years ago. The tax base (EAV) has increased by 6 times over the last twenty years. Two developments, Seven Bridges and Pro Logis Business Park, contribute 22% of the tax base. Twenty years ago, these developments contributed virtually nothing to the tax base. Bond rating agencies have raised the rating of the village.

Quality of Life. The CNS provides the best measure for how the village has performed on "subjective" measures. Here is a brief recap of results for 2008:

- Overall quality of life received its highest score ever for the top rating.
- Residents likewise gave the highest score ever to the top rating for overall satisfaction with police department. Overall satisfaction with the police department has topped 90% since 2000.
- Overall quality of life gets a "satisfied" or "very satisfied" rating from 97.5% of the residents.
- More than 90% of residents since 2000 have indicated that they felt safe and secure in their neighborhoods.

Superior Services. High ratings and continuing improvement characterize the service ratings as well in 2008. Here is a recap:

- The mean rating for dispatcher service, overall agency performance, patrol officer service, response time, police attitude and behavior, and overall satisfaction with the department, all was "Excellent." This is the eighth consecutive year that the police department has achieved excellence on the mean rated score in all areas of service.
- Highest ever ratings were given to public works for snow plowing, street lighting, streetscape, fewest sewer back-ups.
- Bikeways received a positive rating exceeding 95% and the highest ever rating for child bike and adult walking use.
- Village hall customer service received its highest ever excellent rating.

- Commercial area maintenance categories tracking building and zoning performance, including lighting, parking lots, signs, and overall were the highest ever for the top score. Residential maintenance ratings in the last ten years have improved across the board by a minimum of 20%.
- Planning and development department scores got highest ever scores for the top rating in traffic, parking, signage, access, and building design.
- Communications activities led by the administration department obtained highest ever ratings for web site use, quality of web site information, promoting village positives, and residents feeling informed.
- Attendees at the town meeting gave the highest ever rating for the combined score of satisfied and very satisfied.

Stick to the Knitting, But Improve the Pattern

These dramatic performance numbers are a credit to all community stakeholders and how they work together to pursue community building. The focus of the village mission has been steady. The ability to measure the results has given the leadership and the process great credibility. This steady progress has occurred while the mission and goals in Woodridge have seemingly changed in small ways. Those small changes, however, have led to what I think the Woodridge stakeholders would describe as significant improvements—and a collective mindset that the community has positive forward momentum. Citizen engagement has consistently led to two goals of highest priority—a safe and fiscally responsible community. Over the last couple decades the addition of an additional priority generated through the citizen engagement process has been palpable. Let me highlight a few examples of those "small" changes.

Open Space Acquisition. The lead example is the acquisition of the town centre property via condemnation. This open space initiative was pursued because the feedback from our citizen engagement process indicated that this was a community priority. The community also recognized that financial priorities may need to be adjusted.

Senior Housing. I have also shared how the community leadership has responded through the community engagement process to senior housing.

The theme of caring for senior housing needs became clearer as the first decade of the 2000s unfolded. A subtle change was made to one of the housing-related goals to emphasize the need for the community to serve a "variety of housing needs." This change was instrumental in directing staff to pursue an assessment of how the housing stock served the next generation of Woodridge residents.

Include and Support Everyone. Seniors are not the only group to get special attention. The board has also added a goal to facilitate youth service and development. Another addition to the priority goals that we discussed as part of citizen engagement is diversity—improved ethnic and race relations. I see the citizen feedback for seniors, youth, and diverse groups as being closely related. These groups are reflective of a community interest in making sure that all groups are connected to the community and supported to succeed. In chapter 5, I described how we worked to connect diverse groups and youth. In some years the feedback contained a similar theme of "connection," but it was stated in terms of prioritizing activities for community involvement and community commitment.

An Appealing Community. Amongst the many goals set for the community, there is another goal that periodically is placed among the priorities when the board conducts its goal setting session following the multiple sources of citizen. This goal is to improve the appearance and appeal of the community. This goal, ranked amongst the top five priorities five times in the last decade, is often associated with streetscape improvements. Since becoming a tree city in 1992, streetscape improvement is an annual project. Projects include added plantings in the medians, more scheduled maintenance for state and county routes, tree plantings and maintenance of the existing tree inventory, and entry signage. One of the village's early uses of online surveys was for resident evaluation and feedback about the priorities for this goal strategy.

Attract and Retain Top Employees. Not a goal setting session concludes without the elected officials recognizing the work of every employee for moving forward the village's mission. This goal has also received priority ranking in the annual review over the last decade. Retention and development of employees has been an ongoing interest and focus of the board.

Infrastructure Improvement. From time to time, the top four priority goals for a year have included maintaining adequate infrastructure. Woodridge has tried to adhere to a plan for infrastructure development and maintenance that will sustain these facilities. How we settled on some elements of the infrastructure maintenance plan is a story in itself. Let me highlight one example from my early years in Woodridge that also shows the faith and trust that the board placed in the administrator and staff to carry out village goals.

This story starts with the day that I first interviewed in Woodridge. I toured the community before I went to my interview. I don't recall the question, but I did tell that board that my tour indicated the need to improve street maintenance. I drove down one street that was seriously deficient. I explained that Park Forest had a program that maintained all the streets in good condition on a long term basis. When I was hired, I soon thereafter began an assessment of Woodridge's annual maintenance program. I concluded that the program fell short of providing for all the long term maintenance requirements. I shared some of my observations with the board during our annual tour of the village. Driving around the village periodically with your board, and highlighting issues and conditions, is an excellent way to assist board and staff with obtaining "good data for good decisions."

I wanted to build the capacity of the Woodridge staff. I arranged for my former public works director from Park Forest, now a developer/ consultant, to discuss his philosophy with key staff in the public works department. I wanted this former employee to be a resource for my "new employees." I didn't want to dictate a result, but I wanted an exploration of options by Woodridge staff to meet the goal of maintaining infrastructure. The Woodridge public works staff responded positively and began "experimenting" with road surface treatments.

We tried some of these alternative treatments on selected streets—overlays, chip and seal, and seal coat. Following these tests, it was my "good fortune" that we had a resident come to a board meeting before the next scheduled board tour. This lady's assessment of the "chip and seal" option was "not glowing." The street, which was the subject of this scathing assessment, was the same street as a prospective candidate for mayor.

This could have been a "perfect storm." The mayor responded that the board and staff had been assessing street maintenance options and would evaluate the result on this lady's street. We did assess the "appearance" and "feel" of this pavement treatment on our next tour. The board concurred with the resident's assessment that the neighborhood would be more attractive with a higher quality surface treatment. They committed to an overlay for the street.

The board treated the situation as a learning process and took responsibility for the ultimate policy adopted. The mayor and board also supported the "experimentation" with different street surface treatments. They determined the best option for the community—and accepted contributing more money to the final policy decision. The staff had good direction that would require going back to the financial plan and incorporating a significant additional expense, which we did. I see this situation as a prime example of the trust and faith that the mayor and board placed in the professional staff. The elected officials owned the process and the outcome. Woodridge now regularly sees comments in the CNS remarking about how residents proudly know when they enter Woodridge—the streets are better maintained.

Tribute to Strategic Management

The unchanging nature of the village mission and incremental changes to the community goals is a tribute to the steadfast commitment of the village leadership to improving the community through effective citizen engagement. Citizen engagement helps village leadership and professionals identify and forge plans for improving village services and making strides in the quality of life. Routine measurement of performance helps all stakeholders realistically assess progress toward the mission and the "ideals and sacred things" of the city. Mission identification, stakeholder input, evaluation of options, and measurement of results are all part of strategic management and form the basis for how Woodridge works together to build community.

CHAPTER 7

ALIGNING PEOPLE AND ORGANIZATION PROPELS COMMUNITY FORWARD

We have examined the basic values and relationships needed for manager success. We have also looked at engaging stakeholders and developing plans to fulfill the aspirations of the community members. The manager needs to make sure that these aspirations are supported through the daily work of employees who are in turn supported by the resources of the organization. I will identify in this chapter the key parameters of assigning and supporting the mission through the organization and its employees.

Who is in Charge at This Location

Thank goodness for Alexander Haig for leaving us with the memory that "he was in charge at this location" after the Reagan assassination attempt. Alex erred in his interpretation of the line of Presidential succession, but left us with a good example of why we need to know who is in charge. In this case, we better know who is accountable for the mission and goals established by the elected officials. We had to imprint on the organization the principle of accountability between goals and managers and operating units. With the mission and goals set, we needed to begin building the mindset, attitude, structures and network to begin operating on the foundation that had been laid.

We would not have an effective strategy to accomplish the village mission without identifying who was going to take leadership for accomplishing the goals that were set by the board. We needed to identify which member of the management team had responsibility for which goal. We also needed to make sure that each goal had a staff member that was going to take ownership for accomplishing it. Operating leaders and goals had to be aligned for personal accountability.

One-to-One Assignment

I see this process of "assignment" producing a one-to-one relationship between staff leader and goal to be accomplished—all under the management responsibility of the village administrator. Making this assignment could be viewed as simply a formulation of duties and responsibilities. What we really were doing was putting in place the building blocks for a high performing team and learning about teamwork. This was about understanding expectations and perceiving roles much more expansively—more aggressively identifying strategies and action plans that help us accomplish our community building work and understanding that staff leadership is needed to help the team—the community--accomplish its objective.

Aligning Structure with Leadership Accountability

We had to "find a home" for each of the village's important goals and a competent leader to champion and manage programs that would move them forward as part of our mission. Organizations are complicated—just like people. Some of the goals had two departments to which they were assigned. In some cases, two departments that shared responsibility wanted to shift the responsibility to each other. "Code enforcement" was one of the first issues that I identified that needed to be addressed in order to align goals with the responsibilities of members of the management team.

When I was interviewed for the Woodridge administrator position, the mayor wanted to know if I had code enforcement experience. I was able to answer that I did, and I was able to cite several significant cases with which I was involved. When I arrived on the scene in Woodridge, I tried to understand who was responsible for code enforcement. I learned that the public works department housed the building inspection function within its engineering division. Some code enforcement duties were handled by these employees. The code enforcement officer, however, had been assigned to the police department. The code enforcement officer generally worked on complaints related to long grass and junk or abandoned vehicles. Since these complaints often involved tickets and court appearances. The decision was made to rest code enforcement responsibility with police.

This division of duties for the employees specifically assigned to these departments was clear—select tasks were in the hands of the building inspectors and the code enforcement officer had responsibility to persuade people to move disabled cars and cut the grass—or go to court. I quickly learned from conversations with trustees, the mayor, from a couple employees, and my own observations that there was another realm of expectations for "code enforcement" that was not assigned. This category was the maintenance, care, and management particularly of multi-family, and some single family dwellings.

Within the first ninety days of starting the job, I concluded that this category of code enforcement was the most significant area that needed to be addressed. One of the skills and management arenas that I extensively practiced in Park Forest was code enforcement or as we often called it, "housing maintenance." On one hand, I was surprised that I would need this skill in "wealthy" DuPage County, but, on the other hand, I was excited about the prospect for being able to add to the village's capacity to address issues that it faced.

During the next year, we would begin a process of enforcing the codes in a much broader and more aggressive fashion than what had been practiced previously. We would also be moving in the direction expected by the mayor and board and in concert with the mission and goals. The twelve to eighteen month process that we followed was particularly critical to building teamwork, structuring the management team, and establishing long term capacity and expectations for building the community.

This part of the community building process involved three tasks. First, we needed to clarify expectations and the results that were required—align mission responsibilities and team leader. Second, we needed to establish teamwork. People needed to see how individual employee results could be magnified with organization support and interaction. Third, we needed to examine the organization structure that would best perpetuate teamwork and accomplishment of the village mission.

Giving Status and Resources to Important Goals

"Code enforcement" concerns were reflected in three Village goals. First, residents believed that some multi-family areas were not safe and thus diminished our ability to maintain a safe community. Second, the goal of enhancing residential neighborhoods required that homes and apartments which did not measure up to the property maintenance code be addressed. Third, some of these housing maintenance concerns might influence the perception of the community's "suburban image."

In order to illustrate how we addressed these mission-related concerns and to build the "code enforcement" capacity, I will primarily focus on the example of one apartment complex. This apartment complex was perceived by many as ineffectively managed; criticisms included poor screening of tenants and considerable deferred maintenance. During my introductions to some of the police employees, I also heard from some that this was a high crime neighborhood with its share of residents that required police assistance. I started out my own investigation by walking through the complex. I was struck, maybe appalled is a more appropriate description, by the poor conditions of many of the porches and roofs. These were conditions that did not speak well of ownership and management of the complex, nor the village's adherence to its own standards.

Walking Around to Achieve Excellence

Waterman and Peters in their landmark book *In Search Of Excellence* have already documented the benefits of management by walking around. My experience totally supports their conclusion. My first walk through the apartment complex was an eye opener for me. I soon thereafter took the same walk with the department manager responsible for building inspections. He had also served in the position of acting administrator on three prior occasions, so he was aware of some community history and board sensitivities. The department manager readily agreed with my observations of the conditions of the complex. He also shared the perspective that the ownership had been less than cooperative. These conditions had been a key reason that the mayor and board had adopted a policy of not authorizing any additional multi-family units in the community.

After my tour around the complex with the department manager, I next arranged to walk around the complex with the mayor. He concurred with my assessment. I pointed out that the structural condition of the porches might be an effective "hook" from which to undertake enforcement. I told him that the staff needed to look at how we would best undertake the enforcement action. I was sure, however, that it would be a major undertaking. It would be time consuming and expensive. The staff would likely face many challenges that were new to them. This would be a learning process.

At the end of that tour, and for the next five years while we undertook this "code enforcement battle," the mayor's guidance was simple, "If that's what we need to do to enforce the code and correct the situation, then we need to do it. I support it and the board will as well." This is one of many examples of the strong support and encouragement that I received from the mayor during my service in Woodridge. Obtaining that kind of support and enthusiasm from the top elected leader is a basic element needed for administrator success. More importantly, the promise that he made, he kept.

Problem Solving Through the Team

The walks around the complex had me "on a roll," so I decided to continue that as part of the team building process. Since we had at least two departments with some responsibility for this situation, I asked that the managers from those two departments and a couple inspectors accompany me on this tour. You should note that problem-solving conversations no longer involved one employee and one supervisor. Municipal problems often involve multiple departments and many employees. We needed to make sure that problem-solving conversations really involved the responsible team.

As we toured the apartment complex, we once again reviewed the physical condition of the complex and talked about the past attempts to correct these problems. We also discussed the social and policing problems that the community experienced as a result of these conditions. After the walk through, we identified some follow-up work that each team member would complete and put this issue on an upcoming staff meeting agenda.

When we reconvened at the weekly staff meeting, we had additional information and more players—team members—to add to the effort. The weekly staff meeting is an opportunity to inform and educate all the players who are responsible for each function—and to make sure that they all have an appropriate role in the decision making process. We were about to embark on a major initiative and needed to gain insight, support, and contributions from everyone in the room.

As we gathered information on the conditions at the apartment complex, it became clear that we would need to take enforcement action, including a significant complaint before the court. The village attorney is a participant in each of these meetings and he would need to make a major contribution for the village to remedy this situation. We also had the expertise of the village engineer who supervised the building inspection function along with the director of planning and development, finance director, and the assistant administrator. Each of the options for action could implicate these members of the team.

The village prosecutor, who is not a regular participant in staff meetings, was also consulted for approaches to prosecuting the code violations. Her successful experiences in Woodridge have become a foremost part of several books that she has authored on legal aspects of housing maintenance and code enforcement.

Our initial investigation uncovered that the management company was indeed incapable of performing. The complex was actually being managed by this company on behalf of the United States Department of Housing and Urban Development (HUD) which was the receiver (effectively the lender) for the property because the mortgage had been insured by the Federal Housing Administration (FHA). Having experienced this phenomenon in Park Forest, I was not excited by the prospect of dealing with HUD. However, it is what it is! It would be more difficult, but we had an objective to accomplish. The management company, without any forewarning to HUD, declared bankruptcy and effectively abandoned this property and nine others in various communities in DuPage County.

Preliminary evaluation and research of the code violations led us to the conclusion that we had extensive health and safety violations at the complex. The occupancy rate was about 75 percent and we had specifically identified most of these vacant units. While there were risks involved, we concluded that we would put the village in the best position to improve the complex through two steps: (1) "red tagging" or declaring unfit for occupancy the 90 vacant units and (2) filing an action in DuPage circuit court for repair, rehab, or demolition.

It took about two years to win our court battle with HUD. It took another two years thereafter to entirely repair most of the code violations, but the village was also able to obtain a substantial reinvestment in the property through negotiating with HUD to plow rents back into the maintenance and updating of the complex. We also put the subsequent owner into a position to operate the complex effectively and do so from a solid financial base. This truly took some time, but we got a great result. Many of the community problems and challenges that a manager faces will take several years to achieve the desired result. This is a great example of another principle of community building—it is slow and incremental—be prepared for the long term. Stay in your community to see that it is accomplished.

Combine Mission, Leadership, and Resources

I described this case to highlight the three principles of accomplishing results for community building: (1) clarify the mission--that "self-fulfilling prophecy; (2) make sure that you have a staff leader aligned with each goal; and (3) make sure that the organizational structure and resources support the mission and staff leaders. This case also shows the process of team building and structuring the organization for the long term. The complexity of the endeavor becomes clearer when you realize that the "self-fulfilling prophecy" must be "described" and implemented at many levels—inspector to supervisor to department manager to village administrator to elected official to citizen. The city manager needs to be mindful of all these stakeholders and help connect all of them to build community.

The director of public works whose division handled building inspection services ended up being the "point person" for preparing for our multi-family court action. In some manner, we had another six people significantly involved. We took a team action that was separated from the normal structure of the organization. We were pleased with our success and the larger role assumed by many of the employees. I was pleased that I could pass along some of the experience from Park Forest and add to the skills of the Woodridge staff.

The process of "cleaning up" this apartment complex, however, required significant involvement on my part—probably more attention than I could sustain for the long term. This was also not the only apartment complex that required "cleanup." We needed to devote more attention to "code enforcement" and the goals which it encompassed. What more did we do to align our mission, personal accountability, and organizational resources to be more successful in our mission?

We learned some other pertinent information to guide us during our enforcement work at this apartment complex. We found some violations in 1989 that dated back to the 1970s. These deficiencies resulted from the construction plans or staffing to insure that the plans were actually built. Our building inspection capacity had not improved over the past decade. We were on the verge of another building "boom" and we had already seen the evidence of an aging housing stock, if not maintained. We realized that we needed to find a way to control quality of our developments, at time of construction and thereafter, if we were to meet our goals of enhanced neighborhoods, quality affordable housing, a safe community, and sustained balanced growth. The organization structure did not readily provide a match for these goals and an organizational leader for "quality control" who had time and expertise to perform.

Shortly after filing the court action against the housing complex, we began discussions with these same staff members about what organization structure we should design to accomplish "quality control" for village development. This became one of the issues of strategic review during 1990. Which organizational unit—police, public works, or economic development—should undertake leadership responsibility for this function? Should there be a new unit or department to assume this responsibility?

We had learned quite a bit from our first major code enforcement action and taking on HUD. We also learned something about our existing capabilities and the significant skills and demands that would be required to sustain this effort. We probably had six other multi-family complexes that required code enforcement action. What did this burgeoning staff team think about this issue? Despite the recent success in acting against a major code violator, were any of the departments motivated to elevate the importance of "quality control" within their operations, and devote significant amounts of their time to the effort?

Mission, Leadership, and Resources for Quality Control

The planning and development department did not have the capacity or experience in either building inspection or code enforcement. The department also was absorbed in major annexations and developments that overloaded the existing staff. Public works was willing to take on the responsibility, but believed that it would be difficult to raise up the priority for "quality control" above other competing interests of the department. The police chief admitted that code enforcement, as part of the policing responsibility, was perceived negatively by the rank and file. The department simply did not see how code enforcement would benefit "crime fighting" objectives.

The consensus of the staff group was that "quality control" could be best performed by a separate department. This management team took some important actions. First, we worked as a team to solve an immediate problem in the community. Second, we worked as a team to design an organization structure that would better serve the village's long term mission. Third, we had identified how we could match leadership for functional success to each of the goals and strategies important to the village.

Why was this process and redesign of the organization important? It was a great learning experience for all involved to look at how this team took responsibility for organization performance. The role of each individual was expanded and refocused. Expanded roles and responsibilities require everyone to learn and, in turn, pass along this outlook to the rest of the employees and stakeholders of the organization. We will talk extensively in the teamwork chapter about how expanded roles motivate everyone to increase their contribution to the mission.

Isolate the Troublemaker

The city manager can make a difference in forging plans to turn the mission into reality. He needs to follow the first dictum of management-- Isolate the troublemaker! This principle is number one on my list because it is the best gauge to assess a manager's judgment. It is an ideal question to pose when you are trying to make sure that personal accountability is clear and the organization resources are focused on the mission.

Who is the "troublemaker?" Why isolate the "troublemaker?" The troublemaker is the barrier—group, person, issue—that detracts or diminishes progress toward your "self-fulfilling prophecy," your mission. Typically, we might think of an "angry resident" as the troublemaker or the "disgruntled employee" or the "outlying" trustee. We may, indeed, have personal examples that fit these stereotypes. I would suggest that the more common "troublemaker" is better described by the old maxim "we have met the enemy and he is us." The first question that one needs to ask in assessing who to isolate is how I, the manager, contributed to the complaint or concern. Have you supplied the "troublemaker" with the information needed to address the concern? Have you shown a willingness to give the "troublemaker" the benefit of the doubt? Have you done everything needed to narrow the issue in dispute? All these questions help assess the barrier that must be overcome in order to make progress or obtain agreement. Let me first use a concern of a retail developer as an example.

During the credit squeeze that began in 2008, a retail developer suggested that the security, which he had already put up for planned shopping center improvements, was unreasonable and not standard for similar communities and projects. This developer had previously demonstrated a penchant for hyperbole, or at least telling a story that was heavily supportive of his viewpoint. I conferred with the mayor and we agreed that we should collect the facts related to each of his concerns. We did collect that information. As a result, the board modified some of the security requirements and reaffirmed others. The developer was assisted by a reduction in his security.

Once again, good data helped us make a good decision. When we isolated the problem, we were able to avoid either the developer or village being portrayed as the "troublemaker." Small steps like this one help build a city manager's reputation for fairness and credibility. You may need that credibility when a bigger problem arises. Isolating the troublemaker is another practice that helps bolster the trust and faith that is the manager's foundation for success.

CHAPTER 8

DOING GOOD THINGS AND TELLING PEOPLE

Most of us have probably heard the famous line from the movie Cool Hand Luke, "What we have here is a failure to communicate." When projects fail or results are not achieved, "failure to communicate" is often the first rationale that is voiced. I think that communications is too often the scapegoat for other failings. However, it is an important part of succeeding at building communities and it is important to eliminate this as a source, or excuse, for failure. In order to "isolate the troublemaker," you need to effectively communicate. As I often told Woodridge staff, you need to communicate at least three or four times so everyone knows. I believe that you will see that communicating early and often is an essential part of "keeping everyone on the same page" and moving forward as a community. It is crucial to build positive momentum for the community—keep the ball rolling through effective communication.

When Park Forest was selected as All-America City in 1977, the community retained a "PR" firm to tell the story about the community's accomplishment. Some folks involved in the process needed convincing that an outside firm was necessary. Representatives of the firm made one argument that has remained with me ever since. The argument was posed as a question, "What is the definition of PR? Doing good things and telling people about them." This is good advice whatever your role in the communications process.

I regularly shared this axiom with my staff. Sometimes they were reluctant to get the word out. If they had effectively performed the task, they considered their job accomplished. Communicating about a task accomplished might make it look like they were "tooting their own horn." The community likes to know about good things being done; so does the board and employees. Everyone likes to learn about, and be part of, a group that is accomplishing its tasks.

This axiom of "doing good things and telling people" is very simple and, when you think about it in the context of building community, it is very powerful. The positive momentum is contagious! I understand that some of the reluctance for "PR" may be related to a perception of being "slick" or "spinning" a story or relying on a professional firm. You absolutely must prove that you are authentic and genuine to demonstrate, and earn, trust and faith in those with whom you are building community. In the remainder of this chapter, we will see how you communicate to many people, through many people, and do it often in order to get out the good news.

Just Follow W

Communicating in the municipal setting is a classic W issue—and I don't mean George W. This is a case of who, what, whom, and which. Who is communicating? What is the message? To whom are you communicating? Which media do you use? I will be guided by these questions in trying to identify the methods that were employed to "do good things and tell people"—to successfully build community.

Some of what we will talk about is very basic and common sense. Yet these principles warrant reviewing because they are central to effectiveness. I am compelled to take us back to Communication 101. This is the lecture where the professor talks about communication not only being about transmitting information or telling your audience what it is you want them to understand, but also making sure that you listen to their feedback, in whatever form. For you need to know as you communicate, what does your audience know and how are they processing what you are telling them.

As we have come to see on the national political stage, you can't campaign if you don't take the pulse—poll the prospective electors so that you know what they are thinking and, all too often, put the "spin" on your future messages. While I do emphasize relating to your audience, seeking feedback, and taking the pulse, I would encourage being genuine, and not manipulative, in communicating with your friends, neighbors, and the engaged citizenry that is ultimately your objective.

Don't BS the BSer

Trust and faith are built on a foundation of integrity and honesty. Authenticity is critical to success in communicating. People either know when they are being fed "the goods" or will learn later when the projection does not come to pass. When staff members gave me inadequate information to address an issue or had not fully performed the needed homework, they came to expect the standard response—Don't BS the BSer! If you do not have the appropriate information, you are better off communicating your deficiencies and being accurate than giving people information that eventually discredits you.

Communications is Everyone's Job

We will immediately answer who should communicate. Communications is everyone's job. Over the last three decades, I have witnessed and managed a range of organization options for staff support of public relations. I come down on the side of not having a contractor or full time professional on staff devoted to doing the daily public relations/communications. I have had fulltime communication coordinators during parts of my time in both Park Forest and Woodridge.

A full time professional allows the organization to accomplish special communication projects which might not otherwise be done without that devoted attention. However, many key persons in the organization become second row spectators, relinquishing responsibility for routine and special communications, when they believe that they can turn the duties over to the public relations coordinator.

It is best to have everyone in the communications game. The principle of empowering employees and relying upon them to serve and engage citizens as part of their daily contacts dictates that they have the tools to communicate with residents. We spelled out a number of factors that contribute to this empowerment in the chapter on engaging citizens. My principles for communication are an outgrowth of my advice for practicing citizen engagement. Job #1 for employees at the point of service is communicating to the people with which they are interacting and rendering service.

Community events that we initiated in Park Forest, most notably the Scenic Ten Run and Pizzazz, were heavily supported by the full time communication coordinator. These events were hugely successful and may never have gotten off the ground without that full time support. Yet, these events are executed and sustained by heavy commitment of time and resources from one or more operating departments. Woodridge made a major commitment to supporting the Ronald McDonald/Michael Jordan Celebrity Golf Classic at the village's championship Seven Bridges Golf Club. We had third party help and made a major staff commitment. We subsequently hired a full time communication coordinator, thinking that we would gain effectiveness through the staff addition. It did not prove to be more effective and we once again restructured to our initial "distributed PR model." If a community is considering a special event or project, a manager is probably better served by using special project assistance, and keeping all those who support an event or project heavily involved in its implementation and communication. This approach maintains "clean" lines of accountability and is designed to keep employees engaged and fully responsible for their own operations.

While we are on the subject of the Ronald McDonald/MJ Golf Classic, I should mention one of the side benefits of "doing good things, and telling people." The village sponsored this celebrity golf tourney which promoted the village and its championship course. The significant side benefit was to introduce the Seven Bridges development to a party who saw the area as a great opportunity for an ice arena. Woodridge is now home to the Seven Bridges Ice Arena which hosted the USA hockey team in 2009.

Woodridge, like most Illinois municipalities, did not have the luxury of employing a full time public relations professional when I first came to town. We established a communications plan to guide all operating departments in putting together releases, advertising, publications, newsletters, and events. I imported this communications plan from my days in Park Forest, where we placed a higher priority on staff and consultants devoted to public relations.

During my time in Park Forest, we also had a presence on the board of a significant number of public relations professionals who did this work for a living. As with any other municipal issue, a manager should expect more input from your board members when they are subject matter experts or otherwise familiar with the topic. You might even, very carefully, seek their individual input. Thus, by the time I arrived in Woodridge, I had a communications plan that had gone through several "updates" during my time in Park Forest. The stated purpose of the plan is "to promote a uniform, positive identity to residents, employees, businesses and other consumers of village services." This plan is an important part of forming a structure for communications, and part of educating and motivating everyone to participate. In fact, once that education has occurred, departments will be ingenious in getting out the message.

Don't Believe Andre—Image Isn't Everything

You may recall the Canon commercial in which Andre Agassi, his locks blowing in the wind, intones, "Image is everything." Agassi's claim is often repeated by public relations advisors who implore staff to "present" or "communicate" the positive image of the community. You can not communicate "image." You often hear board members talking about the need for village public relations measures to "present" or "communicate" the positive image of the community. The task handed out to the manager and his staff is to communicate the "positive image" and produce materials for the press that explain why they should be positive. One of my more astute public relations professionals along my career path was able to convince me of the importance of not communicating "image." She argued that you should really be concentrating on sending simple messages. This staff member helped me understand the importance of simple accurate messages and do not BS the BSer!

Factual Messages Produce Impact

Messages that are important in describing key details about your community, educating residents with pertinent information, and highlighting important events and projects must be the foundation for your communications efforts. In Woodridge, we had a host of simple, yet powerful messages that we tried to communicate, such as the "successive years of annual tax rate decline," "abundant forest preserves and open space buffering the community," "award winning schools," "best access in Illinois to municipal golf courses," "full range of recreation facilities," and an "extensive off-road bike path system." Not only is communications everyone's job, but we learn that everyone has something good to tell people.

Over time, it is the aggregate accumulation of those messages that eventually paints the image of your community. Routinely communicating key messages will produce your best results. Communicating results achieved by an engaged community will serve as the foundation for the future reputation of the community—and much of the good story will be told by those residents whom you have engaged. Just think of the math—instead of the mayor or board member or manager telling the "good news" you have thousands telling the story of their positive experiences.

Essentials of a Communications Plan

Woodridge has many activities encompassed within its communications plan that are public relations focused. The plan expands upon who has operating responsibility for various factual messages. The plan also suggests audiences that are to be reached and provides some guidance on which media will be used. A key element of the communications plan is the identification of "trigger events," positive events that regularly occur within the village organization. Each department manager is responsible for drafting a press release, setting up photo opportunities or otherwise seeking media coverage of "trigger events." The public works department, for example, is responsible for reporting the following "trigger events" during one month's time:

- Initiation of construction/maintenance projects
- Completion of construction projects
- Indicators of improved system performance (sewer main breaks, etc.)
- Grants received
- Water main flushing

Special events and "trigger events" are also used to compile a calendar of month-to-month activities for each department for the whole year. Continuing with public works as our example, that department will prepare information on yard waste closing, the holiday reuse and recycling schedule, Christmas tree recycling, and what residents should expect during the snow season and related topics during December.

The intent of the communications plan is to create awareness as to how each unit of the village operation may communicate key messages to our varied audiences. The plan requires extensive involvement by employees in every village department. Each department is encouraged to develop a public relations capacity, either through the department manager or a subordinate who is delegated this duty. The police department has an individual who coordinates all press contacts. The department of administration provides considerable support for each department's efforts. Administration provides periodic training in press release form and drafting, cable television communications, and public speaking. The management analyst in the department of administration is designated as the clearinghouse for all communications activities and will assist in the drafting of any departmental press release. He or she also is responsible for preparing and updating the media contact list that serves as the distribution list for media information. The media list includes contact names, addresses, telephone and fax number for all regional newspapers, radio and television stations.

Use a Variety of Media to Reach Diverse Audiences

Since municipal government must communicate with many audiences - residents, developers, businesses, employees - we employ several publications that serve specific audiences for specific purposes. The *Woodridge Weekly,* which contains information on village meetings, bid notices, and program updates, is published in space purchased in the local newspaper. The Weekly was started in the early 1980s in Woodridge as a way to get out routine information at a low cost to the entire community. The Weekly started in the *Woodridge Reporter* newspaper which, at the time, was distributed free to every home in the community. As the newspaper business has changed, the *Weekly* has been periodically reviewed for its effectiveness as a communication tool that gets information out to residents.

As most people are well aware in this age of extensive digital communication, the newspaper is neither the reliable, nor only, medium to convey the message. The Woodridge hometown newspaper, which was distributed to every home for free in 1990, was only distributed to 1000 subscribers by the year 2000. The number of households receiving the hometown newspaper fell by ninety percent during the decade. Woodridge now prints its *Weekly* through a new local newspaper that is distributed free of charge at a limited number of local businesses. I will return to the need to continuously evaluate the effectiveness of media outlets after reviewing some additional examples of print media that have been used by the village.

Newsletter. The *FOCUS Newsletter* is a quarterly newsletter mailed to each residence that covers seasonal events, basic resident information, and features on important governance issues. For most communities, this publication is the most expensive communication tool that they will use. Its marginal value, especially in a community with multi-family housing, is increased by making sure that the publication is somehow delivered to every household.

Business Newsletter. Another publication used by the village since the mid-1990s is the *OPPORTUNITY Newsletter*. Key businesses, brokers, and developers are kept current about new residential and commercial projects through this quarterly *Newsletter*. Concern is sometimes voiced by residents about commercial vacancies in the various shopping centers. As part of the response to this concern and the broader strategy of the success of balanced development, the planning and development department has also published a *Retail Opportunities Directory*. This Directory is a helpful resource for the village's retail attraction efforts plus it provides a way to track vacancies and address the concerns of residents by making available real world comparative data.

Specialty Publications. The planning and development department also prepares an economic development brochure that covers basic demographics and socioeconomic data for Woodridge and the population in the surrounding area. As a transportation hub for the Chicago interstate system, Woodridge needs to prepare data that demonstrates the benefits of the buying power outside its borders. As we will discuss further in a later chapter, and already touched on throughout the strategic management discussion, economic attraction requires many elements to be successful.

We hear many people extol the virtues of small business development. We are regularly reminded that small business is the primary source of job growth in the United States. For those of us who have toiled in the municipal sector for many years, we understand that small businesses require "hand holding," and the recognition that they don't regularly encounter municipal requirements for going through the development process.

As a result, the planning and development department has produced a Business Resource Guide in which a new business, or a business working with the community for the first time, can turn to find out who to contact for things like permits and licenses and what building and development requirements must be met before opening a business. The new business literally has all the information to familiarize them with steps for business entry into Woodridge. In fact, Woodridge produces dozens of special interest informational brochures and flyers each year aimed at special audiences such as parents who need information on drugs and gangs or homeowners who want to build a deck. For each of our neighborhood dialogue meetings, the planning and development prepares a map showing all projects, scheduled, planned, or suggested by developers, which might impact the neighborhood. Why? We want to make sure that issues that may eventually raise a concern are put out in front of people—three or four times so that everyone knows.

If you examine the work of the municipal employee, you will find that most of the customer interface occurs: (1) in the field; (2) at the service desk: and (3) on the phone. As another example of specialty communication, Woodridge's public works department became increasingly sophisticated and comprehensive in communicating its maintenance activities. For activities and projects that are neighborhood focused, such as tree trimming or street repairs, the department regularly distributes information door to door in the affected neighborhood. The department has expanded this communication link by designing a program that also makes available the services of village contractors to residents in the service area for driveway replacement and tree trimming. This is another example of engaging employees and residents for neighborhood and community improvement. The idea was an outgrowth of town meeting conversations.

Adapt to Changing Times

Let's return to the question of "which" media to use. Getting back to Communication 101, city managers need to assess what audiences are being reached. I will further elaborate on the importance of tracking how media used for communications is subject to change. The success of an organization in its communication efforts is dependent upon assessing that change and adapting to the times. I talked earlier about the Woodridge experience with publication of its *Weekly* in the local newspaper. Over the course of the last two decades, communities who rely on the local newspaper have found the audience shrink drastically. Likewise, an increased number of stakeholders in the community have turned to various digital media (web sites, smart phones, etc.) to gain information and stay up-to-date on what is happening in the community.

Since the beginning of the millennium, Woodridge has relied upon E-news, a weekly message containing important news updates on community activities sent out to the mayor and board, employees, and registered recipients. The number of E-News recipients has grown exponentially since its debut, surpassing the known number of newspaper subscribers early in the decade. The recipients of E-news have varied from 2000-3000 over the last five years, outstripping newspaper circulation. Despite the success of E-News, the penetration of the combined communication media, press and digital, was only about fifty percent of the distribution of the *Woodridge Progress* in 1990. This presents a serious challenge to a community that wants to both stay in touch and engage with its citizenry.

In order to "communicate so that everyone knows" a community must look to additional avenues to inform and engage—even more avenues now that we are in the digital age. The internet, as the example of E-news described above demonstrates, is a current medium by which to get out community messages. Web sites and social networking media are in vogue. However, they don't include all the folks with whom you are building community. I have tried to establish a picture of the diversity of village communication initiatives. It is important to communicate your point three or four times, so that people know it. You also have to communicate through multiple media and multiple audiences. Thus, you need a widespread network to get your message out to the diverse group of municipal stakeholders. The bottom line is that managers have to constantly assess the effectiveness of communications efforts. Be aware of the four Ws—who, what, whom, and which.

Recapping the Four Ws.

We build our communications efforts on two basic principles—do good things and tell people—communicate so that everyone knows. These principles are closely tied to everyone participating in fulfilling the mission ("doing good things") and building community ("everyone knows"). Answering who, what, whom, and which will be a regular part of assessing your communications efforts. The who is that everybody has a communication responsibility. Simple messages that accurately convey information about your community, its services, and the "good things being done" will eventually help all stakeholders understand what kind of community you are building. Everyone is the whom for which your communications are directed. You must determine which combination of media will reach the whole audience. Communications is a basic element of building trust and faith needed to build community.

CHAPTER 9

TEAMMATES IN FIGHTING FOR THE CITY'S IDEALS

Manager longevity and success depends upon two factors—high quality elected officials and an effective management team. The manager does not pick his elected officials, except perhaps when he selects a new community. Even then, he has limited information by which to make that assessment. Thus, the risk for failure is greater when the match between manager and elected officials diminishes. The quality and effectiveness of the management team, however, is largely within the control of the manager. This group, more than any factor, sheds light on the quality of the manager and what value the manager adds to the organization. In this chapter, I want to talk about forming, developing, and nurturing that management team—the department managers and key professionals who serve the village.

Management Team—The Core of Joy in Service

It is people who were my magic elixir during my years of public service. I put the management team at the core of people who provided me great joy in the work setting. The management team is the group for which the administrator is responsible. It is the group that directs the operations of the village on a daily basis. If you want to be fiscally responsible, you better have a good finance director. A community absolutely needs an effective police chief if it wants to be safe. Quality construction is more likely to be accomplished with a competent director of building and zoning. The public works director sets the tone for the level of year-round, long-term maintenance of village streets. How effectively the tax base of the community grows is shaped by the director of planning and development. Any organization that exceeds 100 employees and annual revenues of more than $30 million will function much better with well-managed support functions, many of which are managed daily by the director of administration who also serves as the assistant administrator in Woodridge.

So this management group, six directors in the case of Woodridge, play a vital function in an effectively functioning organization and community. I would also count the village attorney as a regular contributor and key participant in this group. This group was at the core of my joy in serving as village administrator. The core of what I considered to be the most enjoyable aspect of my job. These professionals helped to challenge me, impress me regularly with their ingenuity, and make everyday activities fun.

This management team is also the foundation from which we assembled the passion and commitment of all the other employees in the village organization. This team is at the core of success in village operations and the broader responsibility of building community. This team looks for the solutions and strategies that will attain the goals so intimately cherished by the mayor and board and all the stakeholders in the community. The reason that I put team so high on my list of principles for success is because of the need to shape, mold, and develop this core management team. While the shaping of this team is so critical, I find it difficult to explain all the ingredients that I put into working with, and building, this management team. Most of the credit goes to the directors themselves. I will do my best in this chapter to relate those things that contributed to the Woodridge team.

Life Imitates Sport

I have to share a story of one of the experiences that permanently changed how I saw team, the team members, and what was a key to my job. When I first came to Woodridge, my youngest son Adam was a ball of energy and ready to go into the first grade. The U.S. soccer craze had started in the 80s and Woodridge was a soccer town. You weren't a "normal" kid unless you signed up for soccer. We were happy to sign Adam to the fall soccer season as he began first grade in Woodridge. He played and loved it. We appreciated Adam running around and using up that energy. He was much better behaved after he practiced or played. Of course, one of the Woodridge traditions was that you needed to have two coaches for each team. If moms or dads didn't volunteer, you couldn't form a team. Despite my busy schedule, I was encouraged by our local state representative, who vouched for the value of coaching. I succumbed to the pleas of my seven year old and volunteered to coach in Adam's second year. Besides, you couldn't fail because the Woodridge Soccer Association trained you. I am so grateful for having taken this big step. I took pride in my success as a coach, despite my limited skills.

Blame the Coach—Fire the Manager

My greatest challenge was withstanding the critiques of my son following a practice that didn't include enough "fun" drills or the criticism associated with any loss—after all, it is always the coach's fault. I was able to weather that criticism. The coach did have some limits for game substitutions—all players were required to rotate through all the positions and players had to be rested equally—forcing the coach to see the young players in all the possible roles. Once I understood the game and learned about my players, I was pretty good in knowing how the team would perform in any given situation—some periods would be good, and some not so.

I quickly came to understand that success or failure of your team on the field was closely related to how well your least accomplished player performed—and how the team worked together in support of each other. It was an aha! Experience. I saw that my priority as a coach was improving the players, especially those less skilled and capable athletically. Often times these players demonstrated other pluses—commitment, unselfishness, spirit, and character. This soccer coaching experience made my job as coach, and administrator, a lot clearer. I knew that the team that worked together and maximized the improvement of each player stood the greatest chance for success. The coach—the manager—can make a great difference in the performance of the team. Making the team better is perhaps the primary reason for hiring a manager.

Difference between Good and Great

This relationship between the coach and the players—the manager and the team has been discussed at recent ICMA training. In 2007, a long time after gaining this coaching insight, I journeyed to the Annual Conference of the International City/County Management Association in Pittsburgh. The keynoter the year before Pittsburgh was Jim Collins, author of "Built to Last" and "From Good to Great." His books and related research speaks to how good organizations become great organizations. I attended a workshop in Pittsburgh that built on what Collins had discussed the prior year. To be a GREAT organization, Collins believes that our Mission must be based upon core values. Let's call his core values the core values of management. In my breakout group of five other administrators, and subsequently with the employees in Woodridge, I shared what I considered to be the "core values." My list included three items:

1. Team Commitment
2. Individual Initiative, and
3. Personal Development

This topic, the issue of core values, is not one that we touched upon often in our management deliberations. These values may have been the unspoken bond that brought us together. I believe that these are the values that were lived out throughout the organization during my time in Woodridge. My reasoning for this list of core values is pretty simple. No organization is successful without its members making a commitment to each other. Given the tremendously important obligations that a community commits to accomplish with its residents, we must stress that we have ties that bind and bring us together as a team and community. What works on the soccer field and what we consider important in the city hall are surprisingly similar.

Zonis Leadership Concepts—Passion for Core Values

Marvin Zonis lectures on leadership at the Booth Business School at the University of Chicago. He echoes the principle of many other "gurus" that each person needs to see their work as important and meaningful. The manager must help the employee see the importance of the work that is being done. Zonis also argues that the manager must also be able to show emotion and passion reflective of that work. The manager needs to show passion for the mission, the importance of the team effort in executing that mission, and that each person has a crucial responsibility to take initiative for team and personal success.

The concept of the group supporting the individual, and the individual supporting the group, has been a basic premise of management for many decades. There must be a benefit that responds to the needs of both the individual and group. While group efforts and accomplishments are the hallmarks of success, it is paramount that each individual gets better, and that commitment requires the individual to take the initiative and the group (team, community) to help the individual succeed. Perhaps it is easier to understand the simpler coaching concept learned from soccer. I arrived in the same place nonetheless.

Jim Collin's work on the pre-eminently, successful company in "Built to Last" identified more than a dozen companies that were considered to have visionary leadership and strategies that made them leaders in their industries---outstripping other peers by five times. Those same companies nearly twenty years later would not all be likely to receive the same highest ranking. Merck, Ford, Sony, and Motorola have all experienced significant upheavals, sometimes coping with the prospect of extinction. Likewise, Waterman and Peters talked about companies like the Dana Corporation in "In Search of Excellence." Dana, one of the best companies, in one of the US's premier industries, is today fighting for its survival.

Building a Team is a Long-term, Incremental Process

Organizations that were once visionary, but have now fallen from that lofty perch, provide a valuable lesson. They instruct us as to how we must see the building of an organization that will attain long term success; and how we must nurture core values that breed success. First, you need to see the building of a team (then the organization, then the community) as an ongoing process. I've come to see the process as continuously adding bricks to the foundation. Second, you need to always build upon what you have. I am sure that you've heard some administrators or elected officials argue that "they needed to start over." Start by doing your best with what you have. Third, you must always be improving for the long term. After you've improved your community for ten years, what is your plan to improve for the next ten? Even if your organization remains stable, you have no assurance that your environment will. Just ask those companies studied by Collins or Peters that were national peer industry leaders before the economy became globally competitive. Now that the economy is globally competitive, what should these companies have done beforehand to chart a course more responsive to these changes? Thus, my efforts in beginning team building in Woodridge were directed at helping department managers see how they could make individual contributions to the team and improve the role that they played for the benefit of the entire team.

Expanding Team Capacity to Boost Its Members

How do you expand the role and capacity of the staff in a way that boosts each team member? I will highlight through a story from both Park Forest and Woodridge how the administrator can aid this effort and answer this question. The Park Forest event came about two years into my term as manager. Some of the key staff had been in place for several years. This story is about one of those key staff. He was very talented and highly educated and had lived and worked in Park Forest for his entire ten year professional career. Park Forest, as we talked about earlier, struggled to gain investment to sustain the community. The staff was very diligent about exploring all options to gain that investment. This particular staff member was also quite innovative and creative. One of the more unusual ideas that he floated (no pun intended) was to bottle the water from one of our groundwater wells because it was naturally effervescent—we could sell it as "Park Forrier." While Perrier's market share may not have been threatened, this kind of thinking and staff interplay lead to some useful ideas and lightened the burden of trying to make things happen with limited resources.

This particular department head along with his assistant and I had breakfast in mid-1985. We were talking about our success during the prior two years in completing a number of projects that had languished on the "drawing board" since the late 1970s. This department head's bottom line concern was that his workload may diminish, and he would no longer be able to make a worthy contribution to the village. We didn't have money for one of the projects that we thought could aid business development—installing infrastructure in the industrial park that would establish buildable business sites. A good manager always has a plan, and a couple back-up plans and some good luck.

Two weeks after the breakfast at which the industrial park idea surfaced, I received a call from our local state representative. He wanted to know if we had any project that could be submitted for Build Illinois, a state funded capital program. Of course we did—we needed to install infrastructure in the Park Forest industrial park. The state representative would put forward this project for Park Forest as part of Build Illinois. However, it was not guaranteed and would have to compete with other projects from around the state. Projects, like the Mitsubishi plant in Bloomington/Normal, were the "hook" that Governor Thompson used to sell the Build Illinois capital program and those projects would be first on the funding list. Thompson sold the program first and foremost as a program to generate jobs. We had to construct a project for funding that was compelling. Lt. Governor George Ryan scheduled hearings around the state to find out about other projects that would generate jobs.

Making a Plan that They Could Not Refuse

There was no political certainty to gaining any funding from Build Illinois. We decided that we needed to construct a project, if possible, that could not be rejected. In order to put a project forward that had a high certainty of funding the infrastructure, we needed to (1) gain control of the land in the park; (2) design water and sewer mains to serve each of the parcels in the site, including eliminating eighteen foot open ditches; (3) find business owners who would develop sites in the Park and add jobs to the economy. We were able to accomplish each of these tasks in a timely manner. By the time of the Build Illinois hearings, we were able to present a project that could be developed by the village and consisted of two new businesses with, two expansions of existing businesses, and the prospect of several dozen new jobs. No project proposed in the early months of Build Illinois had better metrics per job generated, nor a higher certainty of fulfilling the objective of the capital funding. We couldn't be refused based upon the comparative benefits, nor were we. The Park Forest staff were committed and dedicated and they found the means and strategies to accomplish the project. This is a key expectation that elected officials and administrators should have for the professional staff. The employees and staff need to find ways to get things done—make things happen.

Making Things Happen—Woodridge Version

We talked in the chapter on community building that results are needed to validate the process for the citizens. Each time that results are accomplished, the capacity of the management team is expanded. My second story again demonstrates these two benefits. When I arrived in Woodridge, I found a long list of capital projects that were without an identifiable source of funding. I suspect a variety of factors combined to produce this circumstance. I talked with the director of public works and the planning and development director about how we might fund the programs next on the priority list. They were willing to defer to the mayor and board for how to accomplish these projects, including raising money to complete the projects. Of course, the issue to which I most quickly became sensitized upon my arrival in Woodridge was the firm commitment not to raise taxes, especially off-limits was an increase in the real property tax rate. The staff needed to demonstrate how the board could accomplish these projects within the desired funding limits. Maybe more importantly, the staff needed to transform the image that they had of their role. Like the industrial park in Park Forest, the Woodridge staff needed to be on the lookout for how to accomplish the projects on the Board's list. The staff role required an expansion of expectations--not only what needed to be done, but how it would be done, especially paying for it without a tax increase.

Expanding Roles--Growing the Team and Building Community

We essentially had to find ways to extend two arterial roads and find ways to fund each of them. We weren't in an unusual position for a local government—we needed millions. These two roads had been part of previously annexed parcels, now slated for construction, or were part of the plan for road development in prospective development areas. I asked the director of public works what options that he thought might be available to address our needs. He thought that the county might be a possible source for meeting our funding needs. Over the prior two years, I was aware that the municipal /county relationship had been "rocky" due to perceived intrusion of the county into municipal land use, planning, and annexation prerogatives. The director of public works outlined which roads the county controlled in the Woodridge corporate boundaries, or immediately abutting Woodridge. He speculated that the arterial nature of the east-west road that served as our southern border might be suited for county jurisdiction.

The director of planning and development came up with another angle to consider related to the county's role in transportation and development activities. The county was proposing to fund road construction through a road impact fee. The area for which we were planning, and for which we held great hope of future non-residential development, was primarily served by three roads. A short length of one of these roads was under county jurisdiction. However, the county stood to gain millions of dollars in road impact fees if this area were to develop as projected by Woodridge. The county was likely to be challenged by developers over the authority and equity associated with this road fee "exaction."

Woodridge staff could understand why these concerns existed. The developer was being asked to pay $1000-2000 per thousand square feet of development—homes, offices, retail. The developer could also be asked, absent a concession in the annexation agreement, to construct the roads serving the development area. Without a commitment from the county to participate in road construction, neither the developer nor village could expect to receive support from the county.

The "busyness" of this time coupled with the lack of "practice" by the staff in aggressively exploring and pursuing what help we could receive, and arguing the village's case did not bring us closer to a long term solution as rapidly as I had hoped. There was much debate at the county level involving developers, municipalities, the county board chair, and various county committees. I reached a point in my guiding the staff examination of these issues at which I felt it time to "nudge" the director of public works to sit down with the county highway engineer to talk about the need for county participation in construction and jurisdiction of that southern border arterial.

I have encountered many situations in my career where the most important role of the administrator is in making a timely push for action. Nearly all texts in the art of negotiation emphasize that timing is so crucial. Traditionally managers see themselves as gatekeepers. If the administrator is the gatekeeper, he certainly should also see his role as timekeeper. I asked the director of public works to move forward on making this contact. The director of public works set up a meeting with the county highway engineer and the meeting was set at my office, so that I could participate, although the director was in the lead role.

Taking the Right Path—or Road to Somewhere

After introductions and pleasantries, the public works director described our situation and the extent of our planning for road development in this developing area. The road that we were targeting for jurisdictional transfer was connected to a county road at its east end and state highway route 53 at its west end. Three different entities controlled the ownership and maintenance of this road. The roadway section that we hoped to be improved measured just over a mile.

The county highway engineer responded to our request pretty quickly. He stated that the county did not have an interest in taking over this road. He went on to say that this road would not be a good takeover candidate, but that the intersecting road in Woodridge might be better suited. We tried not to be too surprised. This option could have great potential, especially because it was a solution for road funding proposed by the county. We maintained our composure---not to appear at all euphoric, maybe a little disappointed that "our plan" was not preferred. "But please, tell us more about your concept and plan," one of us inquired of the county highway engineer. He explained that the link of the north-south road to the county highway system was a much better fit for the guidelines that had been established by the county.

As conceptualized by the county highway engineer, this new north-south county highway link could start at 75th Street, near Woodridge's geographic center and continue south to the county route at Boughton Road and onto Interstate 55, and potentially terminate south of Interstate 55 at Lemont Road. This roadway segment was about four miles long and included a bridge over Interstate 55. A number of details needed to be worked out, including how the proposed roadway impact fees adjoining this stretch of roadway might be applied. We indicated our interest in following up on these details. I personally expressed my appreciation to the county highway engineer.

Eureka!

I encouraged the Woodridge public works director to review the concept proposed by the county highway engineer and begin to work through the details. From a dollar standpoint, this may have been the most productive meeting in which I ever participated. This four mile section of roadway provided prime access to the new Interstate 355 and would help link, and distribute local traffic, to the four interchanges that served Woodridge directly. In our best laid plans, this road was absolutely needed to serve the community and was a linchpin of our early expansion plans to the southerly industrial and business areas around the intersection of Interstates 55 and 355.

In our best laid plans, Woodridge would have to pay for most of these improvements. Over the course of the next ten years, this major arterial, Woodward Avenue, would link 75th Street with Lemont Road. There would be seven separate construction projects pieced together to put this arterial traffic link in place. A few years after that fateful meeting with the county highway engineer, following additional and ingenious machinations by the director of public works and other staff contributors, I was able to sing the praises of how the staff team, led by the public works director, completed this valuable roadway with only $1,000,000 in seed money---although the project cost $10,000,000!

I started out in Woodridge with a simple four part strategy. I needed results. This road project, as part of Village non-residential expansion, was part of the dreaming that had occurred by the mayor and director of planning and development before my arrival. It was one measure of defining a good result. This road project, particularly the financial implications, was at the core of my personal management strategy of obtaining results.

For most observers, these were results to celebrate. I was most gratified by the fact that the public works director had reestablished a broader expectation for his role, and what he could help us all to accomplish building community. He took a huge stride forward in terms of how valuable the team saw him, and what the whole team could accomplish. It was a significant moment in the life and growth of the Woodridge team (and community). Our capacity to succeed and solve problems had measurably grown.

Expect Performance that Fulfills the Prophecy for Building Community

We in the city management profession have for many years been explaining our key to success is "hire good people, stay out of the way, and let them do their jobs." I'm sorry, but that is a lot of "bull." At best, this approach to guiding the management team will yield mediocre results. This approach to letting the professionals "do their jobs" most frequently leads to a manager complaining that his department managers have a "silo mentality." At its worse, it will perpetuate the five year turnover in managers—who have "met the challenges in this community and are moving on to another community."

When I became an acting manager in 1982, I explained to my department managers that I expected them to make operating decisions. Some decisions would require their collaboration and cooperation—teamwork. I wanted them to work together to reach effective decisions that required multi-player input and participation. I would evaluate the choices made by the lead department manager against my expectations for contributions received by, and made to, the management team. If they could not resolve differences amongst themselves, I would be able to make a decision. They might not be pleased with the decision that I dictated, but I had that ability. I would prefer not to have to make that choice, however. Seldom did I have to make those choices.

The manager needs to determine if the department managers have contributed their best collaboration and cooperation to each decision. The manager is the beacon to guide the management team. He or she serves as the primary source to add value to each team member and exhort the team to do the best possible. The manager is the model for team commitment, individual initiative and personal development. What else does the manager bring to the management team?

If you are going to lead the management team and add value, you best bring your passion, enthusiasm and excitement. We discussed what the management team has to cultivate in citizens—the importance and worth of citizen engagement. The manager starts the citizen engagement vision by working with his management team. The manager transmits the responsibility for the "sacred things" of the city and quickening the "sense of public duty" through his management team. If you are going to build community, you better be the prime contractor for building the management team. City management is not a passive business where key people go off and "do their job."

Empowering Employees Who Empower Others

The most important thing that manager can give each team member is the expectation that the department manager can perform the job—in a superior fashion--better than anyone else. The same trust and faith that the board placed in my performance has to be passed on to the management team. This is the first step in empowering the management team.

No One Monkey Stops This Show

I have one practical example for what it means to empower the team—to show your trust and faith. Since becoming a manager, I have been pretty steadfast in going on vacation and saying to my assistant that he or she should "take care of things." "Please don't call," I would say each year as I left. I travelled to the Boundary Waters wilderness area each of my last ten work years. There are no computer or cell phone connections in this remote area. I did not receive a work-related call on vacation during my twenty-six years as manager. The team is especially empowered when it can make every operating decision without the manager. I put into practice the axiom of my first fire chief, "No one monkey stops this show!" You've got to prove that you have confidence in the group to make important decisions without you.

Set Boundaries. The manager must set boundaries if he wishes to empower his department managers. Department managers must be able to make most operating decisions based upon their judgment and that of their employees. One particular experience drove this home clearly for me. This story involves SD 99. It was an issue that I wrestled with because it occurred after the failure of SD 99 to honor its town centre commitments with the village.

From the late 1990s until 2006, the village supplied a school resource officer (SRO) to the district. The high schools were not located in Woodridge, so sourcing an officer to a school in another jurisdiction was somewhat unusual although some district financial support was provided. The Woodridge police department saw several benefits—positive interaction with teens, an officer developmental opportunity, and a case-finding and intelligence link to an age group that generates a disproportionate amount of police activity. The department over several budget years decided to allocate money for this position in its budget.

The department experienced periodic issues in "getting on the same page" with the district personnel who were interacting with the officer. Some officer performance and school supervisory issues caused both parties to suspend the SRO program in 2006. At the height of the land dispute with the district, the police chief was asked to reestablish the SRO program. I was reluctant to provide support for doing so. We were dealing with a group of folks who didn't live by their word.

The police chief thought that renewing the commitment was part of building a new bridge. We cleaned up some of the past shortcomings of the SRO program and confirmed the new parameters through an agreement approved by the board. My basis for providing support for a "new beginning" had little to do with the district. It simply came down to the chief being able to make the decision—to have authority and accountability for running a first-class police operation. The chief was responsible for allocating the resources that his department had been provided. I had several years of steadily improving police service—best I learn from what got me to this place. I needed to show him that I had the trust and faith in him to empower the department to be successful. I am so proud that he helped me to better understand this lesson.

Share knowledge without being a know-it-all. Part of transmitting that trust and faith, truly empowering the team, is to share the insight and experience that the manager has gained from prior experience. The manager's willingness to transmit all the knowledge, wisdom, insight, and wealth of experience to the team is critical to demonstrating his or her personal commitment to each team member—affirming their importance and that the manager has committed his or her support for fulfillment of the highest expectations. Downloading that "wealth of knowledge and experience," however, must be done to add to the resources and tools available to the individual managers and the team, not to displace their decision making responsibility.

Popcorn Popper or Chess Board

A management team that is empowered has to be constantly challenged to expand their capacity and performance. The challenge posed is not just for each team member to do their best, but to call on each team member to seek the best from the team surrounding them, at the management team level and in the departments.

I've had two memorable descriptions of my management style which may help you to understand the mentality that the manager brings to challenging the management team. One of my Park Forest staff suggested that working for John is like being in a popcorn popper—there is always something bombarding you. One of my Woodridge department managers was probably more flattering when she said that working for me was like playing chess—you always need to see a few moves ahead in the game. I take both of these descriptions as positive indications that the department manager understood the need to be prepared and ask questions about how to best do their job. I always have counted as my strong suit the ability to ask questions. The manager has to possess the talent and understanding to ask questions. If the management team can answer those questions, you are building the team.

Critical Thinking is not Criticism

The manager has to share his knowledge and his questions. The ability to apply critical thinking to the problems facing local government is so essential to pass along to others in the organization. Critical thinking, and the brainstorming that was usually associated, is so helpful in making sure that all good solutions are considered by the staff in their operational role and by the board in its policy making role. Remember good data make good decisions. I referred earlier in this chapter to the Zonis lectures on leadership. He makes the point in those lectures that work is the place where people seek "achievement and mastery." The manager who helps all those around him record achievement is the successful manager. Woodridge weekly staff meetings were the primary place to share, brainstorm, and fine tune ideas.

The Woodridge staff meeting was an invigorating, energizing, and dynamic get together. The environment promoted the best in everyone

135

and encouraged problem-solving and creativity. We used these discussions to make sure that we agreed on steps to implement village policy, did the homework needed for upcoming issues, reviewed the list of legal issues, properly documented agenda items, shared concerns that surfaced in the organization, and addressed any conflicts that crossed department lines.

Order the Paper Plates

The staff agenda included perhaps the most critical issue for the management team—tee up. Tee up was designed to make sure that any conflict that crossed department lines was dealt with by the management team. This was not a frequent topic for discussion, but when it arose—it was important. Conflicts that are not addressed by the team often fester and are "acted out" across department lines amongst the employees below the department manager. If the team of department managers does not address the conflict, then the problem will become more serious. This role for the management team was never clearer than when we had a disagreement over who ordered paper plates.

The old village hall had a small kitchen. The facility was largely used for breaks by village hall employees and by the three departments for serving drinks and minor food items for special business or community meetings. Because the kitchen served many needs amongst a diverse employee group, it was not clear who was responsible for cleaning and ordering of sundries like paper plates. Employees in two of the departments in the village hall got into a dispute over who should order the paper plates.

When the assistant administrator (department manager for administration) whose employee was involved in the incident approached the department manager who supervised the other employee in the dispute, the department manager first became indignant, then lost composure. This department manager knew "her employees would have to do the clean-up" because they were "less important." This reaction was surprising, but, unfortunately, explained why the lower level employees were in a dispute. They were just acting out the conflict between the department managers. When we properly saw this incident in its "root cause," or more appropriately "root solution," we on the management team better understood that our prime role was to make sure that conflict was resolved amongst us and not left to fester and spread.

Make it Fun

Critical thinking and doing the appropriate homework leads me right into the next major value-added responsibility that the manager has for building the team—making it fun. If work is fun, it is twice as dear. Municipal government and community building are hard work, but there is no reason that it can not be fun. In order to keep the critical thinking and collecting good data fun, I was sometimes inclined to ask the staff person if they wanted to bet one dollar on their conclusion or fact. I might even suggest a different answer. If I was taken up on my bet, we would assign an "umpire" to confirm the right answer. I usually won! Part of the fun was seeing how long a new staff member would take before they realized that I generally only threw out the offer of a wager if I was nearly 100% certain of the right answer. As time went by, I was able to establish the requirement that the winner of the wager gets one dollar with a note explaining the basis for the bet. I now have a retirement souvenir consisting of a large envelope of one dollar bills, each with a note reminding me of the reason that I received it.

Another example of our having a little fun at the village hall is that no birthday would go by without a celebration. Every birthday was celebrated with a treat and a song led by the village administrator—or newest employee who needed "orientation." These events were even more fun because we worked our best to have the group surprise the birthday "kid." The mayor would join us for the festivities if he were in the building. It was not off limits to ask visitors, including residents, to join us in song. No reason residents should not have fun when they visit village hall.

So the Manager is a Bum—Admit It!

I received a big boost for having fun when I chose the last finance director of my career. She was a believer in the FISH philosophy—be there, play, make their day, and choose your attitude. I not only had a finance director, but an organization development specialist. This finance director was incredibly intense, but she wanted to enjoy the work environment and encouraged others to do so. She was the chief promoter of Halloween celebration—and costumes. I took advantage of her enthusiasm and used support of Halloween as "a cover" to pull out those old costumes out of the closet. I joined the dress up a couple times. My wife and two dogs—the ballerina pug and the chain gang golden retriever-- joined me the last year. Of course, the finance director was ingenious and would not be out done in costume design. One year we had a significant board debate on the policy over funding street lights in the neighborhoods. The finance director showed up for work on Halloween as a street light. That's the year I brought out the old hobo bum costume. I was pleased that the planning and development director had a sense of humor, because Halloween was the day for his evaluation lunch—and he had to eat with a bum. I was even more surprised ten months later when I visited this same establishment with board and staff after the town meeting dressed in my best suit and the server looked at me and asked, "Aren't you the bum?"

The combination of critical thinking and fun, led and supported by the department managers, helped to instill a creative spirit in our entire workforce. Woodridge over the past fifteen years was the only three-time winner of the DuPage Mayors and Managers Conference Municipal Innovation Award.

Having Breakfast with the Fire Chief—A Sure Fire Evaluation Format

The manager has many values he can add to the management team and make that team much greater than all its parts. There needs to be a commitment to taking the time to periodically talk with the department manager about his or her progress, opportunities, and challenges professionally and personally. Park Forest provided me with many valuable lessons. One that I cherish most was the experience and training to conduct evaluations of the department managers. In many communities, evaluations are often high anxiety occasions. Too often the evaluation session is a time to deliver bad news that should have previously been shared or communicated.

I largely was able to avoid these situations. How I learned to make the evaluation a positive, effective development tool is first attributable to my early experiences as a manager, and the relationship that I had with many of the people that were my department managers when I started. Second, I gained valuable input from this group that helped shape the process, my attitude, and the evaluation instrument as I moved on to Woodridge. This subject is so important to the quality and success of the management team, and different from the experiences of many communities, that I need to outline the evaluation process in greater detail.

My long term as an assistant in Park Forest meant that when I finally became the manager that I had the good fortune of having worked with many of the department managers for eleven years. We grew up professionally together. We celebrated holidays together. Many of our children were born in the seventies. My wife was in the labor room for one of the spouses when the husband was absent. When I became the village manager, I had professionals around me with whom I grew up, and had more than a boss-subordinate relationship. Some of these "subordinates" had counseled and coached me during those formative years in my professional career.

The evaluations that I conducted for that original group of managers included what I considered to be the basics of an effective evaluation—tell the employee what they are doing well, and tell them in what ways they can improve. It wasn't complicated. It wasn't comprehensive. Before becoming manager, I had often enjoyed breakfast with the fire chief. I carried this tradition over to my formal evaluations. The setting at the breakfast table, coupled with my long term professional and personal history with this group, made these first evaluations as manager very comfortable and very productive. The setting was congenial, honest, and open. We were able to conduct productive evaluations that were enjoyable professional encounters. I built on this model for my time in Woodridge as well.

Because of the success of these early evaluations in my stint as manager, and the commitment of that management team to produce a model by which to conduct evaluations, we turned our attention to improving the evaluation instrument. After considerable work and several iterations of the template, we developed a form, except for some small revisions when coming to Woodridge, which has withstood the test of time. The evaluation form tries to reflect the full scope of work for which a department manager is responsible. Functional areas are covered—(1) general management; (2) personnel; (3) communications; (4) budget; (5) risk management; and (6) assistance to superiors. A significant portion of the rating depends upon self-evaluation by the department manager for (1) achievement of targets and strategies related to the village's mission and (2) fulfilling personal objectives. The review of functional areas covers all the key areas of managerial skills and performance. The review of achievement tries to balance how things are achieved against what is achieved—process v results.

A couple of the areas of the evaluation are worthy of some elaboration. The assistance to superiors area has come to signify and reflect those areas in which the department manager has (1) stepped forward to take a lead position for important policy issues or projects and (2) shown leadership responsibility for development of the management team. The personal objectives are those targets set by the department manager by which to improve personally, but not work related.

Evaluate Your Golf Game.

This measure to evaluate fulfillment of personal targets was suggested by an organizational development consultant that we relied upon in Park Forest and who conducted that team building session which I described in my first months in Woodridge. I was somewhat skeptical about including a non-work related measure. The consultant said that it would open doors to unexpected results. I am still a bit amazed by the results produced by that suggestion. Some department managers chose reading more books as their personal target; others wanted to learn golf.

Especially since the late 1990s, I have found this measure a great entrée to talk about ways to aid individual improvement, especially for work-related issues. This measure has been the lever from which to discuss one of the big issues of the day—life-work balance. Because this standard was in the evaluation instrument, I have talked with many department managers about how I can help them accomplish their targets for more quality personal and family time. The employee, his or her family, and the village have benefitted immensely. The subjects we have discussed have been wonderful reminders to me how I could be a better husband and father.

If you are a manager, and don't enjoy your periodic evaluation sessions with your team members, then you are not doing it right or are in the wrong business. I found that the time that I spent in semi-annual evaluations with the department managers is one of the most enjoyable occasions of the year. The tone of the evaluation needs to reflect that joy and celebrate the relationship that you have with each department manager and the joy of the team. The atmosphere should generate a free-wheeling discussion of successes, challenges, disappointments, and dreams. These evaluation sessions, which require about five hours of preparation, often last three hours and welcome a full exchange of viewpoints.

Hire Good People

Another brick in the foundation of manager success is to "hire good people." Good people are more than technically competent. They are more than good presenters. Good people are more than smart. John Adams, our second President, described the right person as a "skilled person with principles." If Adams meant principles <u>and</u> values, then we are in agreement on the right person. Good people are people who understand building community and public service. Good people are those who understand that it is all about community, and not them.

The situation that I found in Woodridge when I arrived held so many positives. One of those positives was the people who worked there. The public works director was just one example of the existing employees who had an understanding and history of commitment to the organization. The first corollary to hiring good people is to put your trust and faith in the employees who preceded you—embrace them as though you hired them. These employees are your best chance for short term success—for the results that you need to produce to get off to a good start.

Admittedly, the department managers must prove themselves. Give them the opportunity. The new administrator must also prove himself. You both have job security motivations that mutually cement your relationship. If a department manager is not performing acceptably, you will eventually learn about the shortcoming. Others in the organization may have known before you, because you are the "new kid on the block." When you do find a deficiency, you will need to address it. In the meantime, you have a more important value to demonstrate to the organization who is watching. You need to show your fairness and best expectations for those whom you manage. Make the best out of the team that you inherit.

Means--Hire Good People

One principle that stands out when I look back at the employees that I have hired over the last four decades is that they are good people. I always felt more confident in a hiring decision when the prospect had some enduring quality for how they conducted their personal life. Did they evidence the good works and community involvement in prior activities that showed their commitment to the people in the world around them? I can point to several examples for the managers with whom I have worked. One was named the outstanding volunteer for high school athletic activities. I had lunch before my retirement with the first public works director that I hired back in Park Forest. He explained his current efforts to raise food and money for a local food pantry. His Monday evenings are now devoted to serving a meal to the needy at a local church. To reach a better hiring choice, be sure to look at the character of the prospect and how his or her activities reflect service, including special efforts to community and family. Those qualities of service will be displayed in the community after you hire them.

Hire Someone Who Enhances the Team

My perception of the hiring process for key management personnel has changed markedly over my career. I want to highlight particularly how I see that the role has changed and what I consider to be the two most important areas for the manager to be involved. The current day manager has much the same authority as his predecessors—the final hiring decision rests upon the manager's outright approval or recommendation to the corporate authority. The first action that I strongly encourage the current generation of managers and administrators to follow is to permit significant input to the employees and management team in recommending candidates for hiring.

When I interviewed for the village administrator position in Woodridge, I was asked in what area I could do a better job. I admitted that I had not been satisfied with some of my recent hiring choices, and hoped to be more effective in the future. Under the Woodridge village code, I was aware that the administrator had less authority over the final hiring decision of department managers. The Park Forest manager who had greater authority under the statutory referendum form of government experienced much questioning of his decisions. So I examined my role in Woodridge from the standpoint of differing authority and the need to improve the outcome based upon my role and input.

Don't Rush Important Hiring Decisions

With the responsibility for personnel hiring decisions squarely on my shoulders, I needed to find the formula for success. Having had experience with some department manager hires that did not perform up to expectations, I chose to invite more input and additional assessment from those around me. With each subsequent choice that I faced for hiring a department manager in the early to mid-90s, I decided to get more opinions from the members of the management team. I eventually reached the point where I withheld a final decision until after the hiring team gave me a recommended candidate. Given my commitment to the team and its prominent role in steering the organization toward the village mission, I probably was overdue in implementing this action—this act of faith in the wisdom of the group.

The other factor that helped me immensely in improving the people that I hired was to thoroughly review and evaluate the track record of the prospect. I would do most of this personally. What had the person about to be hired accomplished? What impression has he or she left behind in the community where they worked? The police department can provide some basic investigatory background. I needed to <u>hear</u> from the people "live" who had direct contact with the prospect. I needed to understand the energy, persistence, and public service contributions. I needed to understand firsthand how the candidate ignited the passion for service in persons who encountered the candidate in other workplaces or arena I needed team members who had a clear history of results, including projects completed, leadership provided, and a history of team contributions.

I would jokingly comment after doing this background procedure for several management hires that I would not choose a person unless I had eight pages of positive comments. The shortfalls in managers that I hired earlier in my career were often made because I placed too much urgency on getting the position filled, and finding someone to do the "work." I learned that I can find a way to get the job done on an interim basis in other ways—contracting, reprioritizing, and asking people within the organization to help. My best advice is do not pick someone until all the indicators support long term success. It sometimes requires patience, but it has a tremendous payoff.

The Lombardi Team

Sometimes you have to go with what you know. I grew up near Green Bay in the 1960s. The Woodridge mayor is a lifelong Packer fan and season ticket holder. I like to think of our efforts in Woodridge as inspired by, and akin to those of the Lombardi Packer teams. I ask forgiveness of the Bear and Viking fans that worked with me over the years. I only make the reference to Lombardi and the Packers to show the high regard for which I hold the management team. What are some of the traits that make the team a champion?

First, the top management team must understand their purpose. Simply stated, the team member must always be cognizant of the mission. Woodridge has a mission that, when stated in its simplest terms, requires the team, the collective core management group to take responsibility for steering the organization toward its mission. This responsibility is superior to the department or functional duties of the department manager. It requires that decisions and choices be seen for how they impact the "big picture."

The department manager must first weigh the impact of his decision on the community. Department employees look to their department leader to act as their advocate. This role requires that arguments be put forward to gain more resources and improve the conditions and status of the department. On the other side, the department manager who sees the "community" perspective may determine that his department's request has a lower priority than a proposal of another department. Evaluating the priority against the village's mission becomes a powerful educational tool.

Why an education tool? Traditionally, the department manager is expected to develop all the arguments and tactics to make the best case for his or her functional area. In the successful team environment, the department manager must also be able to explain how this solution or allocation of resources best accomplishes the village mission. Each team member is expected to learn and, hopefully, understand how each element of the plan builds community. The team begins to act collectively with unity and a mission-focused purpose, because it thinks collectively with a mission-focused purpose. The village administrator needs to play the lead role in encouraging, guiding, cajoling, and demanding this type of thinking and action by each member of the team.

The department manager assumes greater status for his or her department by becoming a functioning member of the management team. Team members take on special responsibilities in their roles. Each member must become a leader within, and outside, the organization. If the village administrator is going to successfully tackle the full range of municipal issues, then he will need to count on team members to play a lead role. I used to jokingly hand out these expanded lead roles by introducing the new "czar." A "czar" has a big job. The additional responsibilities and status for the department manager usually have profound consequences for those employees closest to the manager—like greater exposure for each employee as an architect and analyst for the expanded role of the department and its manager.

The department managers are not expected to abandon support for their areas of functional expertise because they become team players. They need to lead their operating units as effectively as possible. They need to begin to tell the story about how their departments play key roles in fulfilling the village mission. Department managers must expand the roles of many subordinates, and in doing so, raise the stature of those employees. Successful village organizations always have an opportunity to spread the circle of those who are working to build community. The new and expanded role of the department manager on the leadership team is an extraordinary stepping-off point for the team to engage more employees.

Department Manager Promoted to Czar

I will share one shining example of how the "czar" of electricity, the public works director, enhanced the department through his leadership on behalf of the entire community. The public works director became the electricity "czar" after a series of power outages repeatedly shut down businesses in our largest business park—the third largest in the Chicago area. The businesses affected by these outages suffered significant product and productivity losses. The village's business development efforts were suffering as was the village reputation for being responsive and making things work. Of course, the village stood to lose significant revenue from property, utility, and sales taxes.

The public works director took the assignment and produced remarkable results. He immediately began collecting data and working to "isolate the troublemaker." The electric utility did not take responsibility, but blamed other companies working in the village and utility rights-of-way for damaging electric feeder lines. The public works director worked with his engineering staff and field inspectors to immediately record and investigate all outages. This department team established a protocol to assess each outage, assemble all involved parties, and determine the responsible party within twenty four hours.

The public works director and his staff had collected substantial "good data." The director appealed to the electric company vice president, who he knew from his church, to get involved. The mayor and I conferred on a plan and, along with appropriate village staff, met with the utility and all interested businesses. As a result of the excellent work of the public works director and his staff, the mayor obtained commitments from the utility to reimburse businesses for their lost product, supply a large generator to serve the park, and construct bi-directional feeder lines to increase the power capacity to the business park.

The success of the "czar" of electricity was also a success story for the department and all public works employees who directly and indirectly became involved. The capacity and expertise which the department gained from this experience has enhanced its value in the development process and its partnership with the planning and development department. Our engagement of businesses in the industrial park to improve electricity service has led to their involvement in other village endeavors, including the community pantry. Several businesses have expanded within the park because the village has increased the responsiveness of major utilities to customers in Woodridge. These businesses have provided unsolicited testimonials to the mayor for the village's efforts and have encouraged other businesses to locate within the community.

Engaging the Organization—Bottom to Top

If it has not become abundantly clear, I will again clarify an important theme that is part of understanding the role of the manager. Community building needs to be a team approach. The team can never be too big. The more people on the team, the better the result. The manager needs to help connect the dots—the players. We talked earlier about forging the connection between employees and citizens. I want to cover engaging employees from the standpoint of also connecting the employees, especially starting with mid-level professionals and supervisory staff, to the department manager team. If you want this group to meaningfully participate, then you must give them significant duties.

There is a substantial role for middle managers built in to the strategic management process. Mid-level managers participate beyond the department level at four junctures in the process: (1) informal preliminary budget discussions; (2) budget insight meeting; (3) triple I; and (4) budget workshop. The greatest progress that I saw in the organization during my two decades in Woodridge was in the ranks of mid-level managers, much of it due to the meaningful role accorded this group through this process. Let me highlight through two examples the growth and value added by increasing the role and capacity of the mid-level managers.

The public works supervisory staff had limited participation in budget meetings when I first arrived in Woodridge. When they participated, the role of the supervisor was to provide a "pitch" for a piece of equipment or a change in process that was tied to their experience or anecdotal evidence. We sometimes were able to support the supervisor's proposal, and sometimes not. The budget choices that we made had mixed outcomes from an effectiveness standpoint. The public works supervisory staff today has new proposals and improvements each budget cycle—they show the way in doing more with less. They relish questions during each budget meeting. You ask them a question and they are prepared to answer—along with historical data, cost-effectiveness analysis, and implications for related operations. The transformation of these supervisors has been nothing short of amazing and their contributions outstanding.

My second example is the police supervisors. In the first half of the 90s, we had arrived at the time in the budget process where I asked for adjustments to meet the village's targets for the five year financial plan. The police department had proposed a new canine unit. I'm sure that I was not convinced of the value that a dog would bring to police work. I was reasonably certain that the canine would be pared by the department when we made additional budget cuts. I distributed the amount of "budget adjustments" as we began our "feeding frenzy" lunch. The police department staff worked feverishly to trim the budget.

I was utterly amazed when they delivered their cuts to me and prepared to depart. The canine unit was not on the list of reductions! The finance director questioned what I would do. I explained that five members of the police department had worked diligently and fulfilled our request. The final package that the police department management team proposed included a canine unit. The department team was strongly committed to this budgetary outcome—committed enough to make sacrifices in other areas of their budget. We accepted their budgetary recommendations. The police department performance has benefited on numerous occasions by this budgetary decision and continues to do so. Had the police supervisors not so effectively crafted the budget proposal, we may not have had such a positive outcome.

Replacing the Boomers

There is in our midst great anguish and consternation about the next generation. Are they committed enough? Will they step up to the plate? Will they be prepared to face the challenges of community building? I know that the younger people (as my career proceeded they eventually all were younger) with whom I had the good fortune to work were on the track to be outstanding professionals.

Masters of Important Work

The managers who practice what I have shared in this book will discover that they don't have to do "succession planning." Give important work (mission critical) to good people (impassioned for public service) and empower them (trust and faith). You will have a line of outstanding employees waiting to serve your community. Many of the employees in our communities want to be masters of important work. Those employees deserve support because of their (1) commitment to the team; (2) individual initiative; and (3) personal development.

I have frequently faced the question of insider or outsider in filling a department manager position. This choice is one that managers are most likely to encounter in the police department. Earlier in my career, I opted for the outsider, thinking that the outsider brought additional skills and a perspective to the organization that was previously lacking. I know—never say never—but I now consider the odds strongly in favor of promoting an insider whenever possible. If you do not have a strong internal candidate, you best look in the mirror and ask yourself—why not?

Woodridge's prospects for long term effective professional management are strong. The line-up of existing department managers includes one over fifty, two who turned forty in the last year, and two in their mid-30s. All the Woodridge department managers rose to their position through promotion from within. The new village administrator is my former assistant. Woodridge's current employees include one out of every three who occupy their current position as a result of a promotion.

Woodridge Staff Engineer Coup d'état

Shortly after my retirement announcement, I sat down with my assistant and shared with her my perspective on the transition, including my prior experiences and what support that I would provide in my last six months. I was, at first, surprised to learn that the department managers had already talked about the transition. They had decided to meet monthly for lunch and discuss how they could work as a group and face the special challenges ahead. The administrator—me, their key supporter and number one admirer—was not invited. They needed to work as a group that would continue to build the community.

For a few moments after learning about my exclusion from this special monthly transition management team meeting, I was disappointed. I like to be included. I quickly remembered the advice that I received from my good friend John Fontana. You know that you have succeeded as a manager when the people you leave behind are so competent that they can do it without you. I have complete trust and faith that this team will continue to produce success for Woodridge.

CHAPTER 10

BUILDING THE COMMUNITY OF TOMORROW

This book has tried to describe the essence of building community. Why we do it and how we do it. City managers have a variety of paths by which they enter the profession and a wealth of circumstances that bring them to the profession. Hopefully, city managers understand that the "ideals and sacred things" of the city are their ultimate goal. Pursuing this paramount objective must be embedded in basic values of trust and faith, integrity, and respect. Joining with elected officials, the city manager can facilitate citizen engagement that will help the community focus on its mission. The unity and clarity of purpose shared by elected officials, citizens, and employees will produce exceptional results in achieving the goals and mission of the community. Build a strong partnership with the mayor. This partnership is the basis for nurturing the teams, board and department managers, that will help link the entire village organization with citizens. Communicate to everyone participating in order to inform, include, and educate. This is my guidance for successful community building.

I want to conclude my perspective on community building through a few personal observations. My first personal commentary will cover experiences—"good things"-- that have left their mark on me and may provide some additional insight into why we are motivated to public service. My second group of comments will cover personal concerns about the future of our profession and, more accurately, democratic governance.

Finally, I will close with a personal experience that brought special meaning to my work.

My List of Doing Good Things and Telling People

I have spent a career encouraging others to "do good things and tell people." I've had the time to ask myself what I would put on that list to tell people. I am surprised by what first comes to mind. Some of the experiences on my list may also say something about the kind of people attracted to our profession. I have already described some of the experiences that have moved me. I would single out two more experiences.

Very Personal Experiences

The first experience involves an employee that I hired in the late 1970s, when I was immersed in personnel activities and not yet a manager. This employee was hired under a special federal jobs program during the slow economy of 1978. He was well educated, but had experienced a couple unfortunate job losses. His job performance did not meet his educational capacity and at times was erratic. We soon discovered why he was having difficulty retaining a job. He was an alcoholic. With the support of his supervisor, we worked on a plan to help him rehab. This employee enjoyed a successful recovery. He worked for several more years before retiring. He was immensely grateful for having the support to turn his life around. I am immensely grateful for having the opportunity to help him.

My second experience was working on bike paths—more precisely a couple bike path projects. I was involved in acquiring part of the Michigan Central railroad right-of-way in Park Forest, as part of a thirty mile Old Plank Trail. I also had a role in bike path development in Woodridge, including the Woodridge section that travelled along the I-355 extension. These projects go a long way toward connecting the west suburbs to the south suburbs--about a fifty mile stretch. We will soon be able to go from northern DuPage County to Woodridge to Park Forest to northern Indiana. I had a small part in helping to make this happen at a couple stops along my career path.

I have contemplated why these items ended up on my "doing good things" list. My first explanation is that we all feel better about ourselves when we say that we can help someone else. The isolation to which managers are often subject is diminished when we can see a visible, very personal result from our work. It is something that is real; that we can touch and feel. Second, both these examples make the work of community building very real. I helped an employee who helped make the community better. I contributed to building links in a path. The path now goes farther and to more places than I would ever have expected. Third, I see these two experiences as small contributions to a lifetime of building communities. These experiences stand for the thousands of small contributions that people make to each other and to building their communities. The result to me is simply amazing.

Career Accomplishments

My list of formal career accomplishments can be summed up as contributing to building communities in which I have great pride. There are a few components of building those communities that give me extra pride. I would put those accomplishments in four categories: (1) fiscal responsibility; (2) diversity; (3) supporting top quality people and organizations; and (4) sustainability.

Fiscal responsibility. This component is a result of being a good steward and continuously looking for ways to bring greater value to community services. A major element of this achievement revolves around making sure that long term needs are properly addressed and financed. The game, especially at higher levels of government, has increasingly become how you shift financial responsibility to future generations.

Diversity. The future belongs to communities that can include everyone. The ideals of inclusion and respect are the essence of building successful, diverse communities. I am extremely proud of the commitment that Park Forest and Woodridge have made to be leaders in achieving this. The whole is greater when everyone participates. I took comfort and inspiration from my music group at Saint Scholastica and one of our favorite songs *We are Called*:

> We are called to act with justice.
> We are called to love tenderly.

We are called to serve one another,
to walk humbly with God.

Supporting top quality people and organizations. I have worked with so many wonderful, capable people. The organizations that I served distinguished themselves because of the mutual commitment of all the participants. I was so much better for having worked with people who were committed. I proudly have supported them in their efforts to build community and gain joy from public service. I have gained so much more from them. They have helped me understand that I can always learn more from the contributions of others. They have taught me how to put life in perspective. The elected leaders are an inspiration for doing the right thing for their community.

Sustainability. We have focused on building community. One element of building that community is that a community is able to work toward long term goals and pursue its mission—that capability is ongoing. That is sustainability. I have done my best to make sure that when I left Woodridge as the administrator that I left behind capable people, processes, and values that will sustain the community. I plan to stay and build the community in my future role as engaged citizen.

The Future--Democracy in Danger?

Politics at the national level over the last decade have become increasingly polarized. The notion of "greater or public good" espoused by the 18th century political philosophers, translated into the Declaration of Independence and eventually the Constitution and Bill of Rights, seems to be a concept that is becoming increasingly distant. "Politics" is the overriding consideration. Who wins the next election, and oftentimes the public perception in the blogs, is a matter of utmost concern. The battle of daily public perception has filtered down to state and county levels of government. In too many cases, we are becoming government by press release and blogs, designed to generate favorable sentiment without informing and educating citizens.

I am sure that local government has already been infected by this malady. Democracy certainly is predicated upon voting, succeeding or failing at the ballot box. I know of no option better than democracy. I know that democracy, however, will thrive best where it relies upon an educated and involved citizenry. My fear is that the mode of operating at higher levels of government will destroy the coming together of people at the local level to build community.

This failure of federal and state governments to promote problem solving and educated deliberation produces inefficient and ineffective policies and threatens to erode our national resource base. Over the last three decades, the state and federal governments have increased their consumption of resources leaving less and less available for local government. The current US financial crisis will further erode the economic base of local government.

Good Luck—You Will Sometimes Need It

I've described a number of events in this book that I have experienced and how they have influenced my life. Literature on any subject is filled with the opinions of "experts" and their principles. If you met me, I would probably be talking passionately about city management at the first opportunity. I would soon be probing whatever the issue with questions. Soon into our discussion, I suspect that you might notice a definite bias toward the values and principles that I have shared with you.

I am not a person without opinions about the "right" way to do something. I have not, however, placed enough emphasis upon the value of good fortune—good old-fashioned luck. I have been blessed by being in the right place at the right time. I was probably fortunate not to be selected for a couple "dream jobs." Many good, capable, skilled people practice the profession of city management. Some are not given the opportunity to perform; others may be in a no-win situation, unable to fulfill the reality of often competing and contradictory expectations from their boards or communities. To each of those persons, I salute their enduring effort and commitment to building communities.

Make the Community Your Hometown

There is always a personal story behind every dream. I'm no different. My dad came to visit me in Park Forest several years after I started. He had a wonderful grasp of life and people, but was the prototypical man of few words in his family interactions. He seldom left his world in Two

Rivers. He was a model for love of community. I was never too sure what he thought about my own accomplishments, not critical, but also not affirming. I guess that he was a typical "greatest generation." He was always quietly supportive.

During his visit to Park Forest, we went to the local Jewel store to pick up a few groceries. I am the family shopper. As we went through the store, I greeted the employees at the deli and the meat area. I encountered several residents as we walked the aisles to which I introduced my dad. As we exited, I met another resident who had a more detailed inquiry. I finished with the resident and walked with my dad to the car. As we got in the car, he looked at me and, with a definite look of satisfaction, said, "This is just like Two Rivers, you know everyone." Ever since, I have taken that moment as the affirmation of my life's work. His comment meant that building community and a place to carry out life's purpose—the ideal and sacred things of the city—is a dream worth pursuing.

LaVergne, TN USA
02 June 2010
184623LV00002B/3/P